Thoughts Matter

Thoughts Matter

The Practice of Spiritual Life

MARY MARGARET FUNK

O.S.B.

Foreword by Kathleen Norris

CONTINUUM • NEW YORK

1998

The Continuum Publishing Company
370 Lexington Avenue
New York, NY 10017

Printed in the United States of America

Library of Congress Cataloging-in-Publication Data

Funk, Mary Margaret.
    Thoughts matter : the practice of the spiritual life / Mary
Margaret Funk ; foreword by Kathleen Norris.
        p.   cm.
    Includes bibliographical references.
    ISBN 0-8264-1063-4
    1. Deadly sins. 2. Spiritual life—Catholic Church. 3. Catholic
Church—Doctrines. 4. Cassian, John, ca. 360–ca. 435.   I. Title.
BV4626.F86   1998
248.4'82—dc21   97-51620
                                                                 CIP

Grateful acknowledgment is made to Terrence G. Kardong for permission to quote from his *Cassian on Chastity: Institute VI, Conference XII,
and Conference XXII*, Introduction and translation by Terrence G.
Kardong, copyright 1993.

Contents

Foreword

I wish that this book had been available to me fifteen years ago, as I was just beginning to make my way back to the Christian Church. Like many in the "baby boom generation," I had drifted away in my late teens. And as I ventured to return, one of the most valuable things I encountered was the world of the fourth- and fifth-century desert monastics, including Evagrius and John Cassian. They provided me with a sane, healthy religious psychology that allowed me to reclaim and reinterpret something that since my adolescence had seemed irredeemably negative in the Christian tradition, the concept of sin.

Sin had always seemed like a grocery list of "do nots." Some sins, like greed, didn't often surface as an enormous problem for me. Lust had led me into temptation, and real trouble at times. But the theology of sin itself, at least what I had gleaned from my conventional Protestant upbringing, was next to useless for living my life as an adult. It was only when Evagrius and Cassian got me to look at my ordinary "thoughts" and where they led me that I could begin to appreciate the profound and livable wisdom of a tradition that I had long thought outdated and irrelevant.

This book is one of several recent works focusing on Christian life as a practice. (Another is *Practicing Our Faith*, edited by Dorthy Bass.) I find Meg's work to be especially refreshing at a time when so many Christians seem to be setting aside what is best in their own tradition and shopping around for spiritual relief in the worlds of psychology (and sometimes psychobabble), New Age spirituality, and other religions. Not that any exploring is bad in itself. But I am relieved to find a Benedictine woman making so strong a case for touching home base, as it were, for employing the basic spiritual practices of the monastic tradition.

Although talk of "desert monks" may seem exotic, the good news about the practices of meditation and renunciation that Meg speaks of in this book is that they are open to anyone. Learning to "identify one's thoughts" as a Christian practice might very well complement what one is learning with the help of a psychiatrist or therapist. The sort of contemplation and discernment described here might appeal to someone who is involved in Centering Prayer or Buddhist meditation practices. A young mother or father, a single man or woman, might find this book as useful as would any monk or nun.

Above all, this little book can help to give people a grounding in a prayer life that is not narrow, pietistic, or self-centered. In converting our way of life by the means John Cassian recommends, and which Mary Margaret Funk has interpreted in a contemporary way, we soon discover that to remain stuck in the self, and in the therapeutic, is nothing but a short-circuit. Christian prayer demands that we fulfill Christ's great commandment, and in employing the practices of traditional monastic prayer, we find that we soon reach outward from the self, to Christ, and to our neighbor.

Jesus has told us that we contain within us the reign of God. Another Gospel text that we might read in connection with this book is the seventh chapter of Mark, in which Jesus also reminds us that we contain a myriad of thoughts that rise up out of our hearts, like little blips on a radar screen. It is those idle thoughts—"Gee, I hate that guy!" or, "If she weren't married, I could have her," or even, "I've been fantasizing all morning about that cake; I'm going to eat the whole thing"—those seemingly little devils that can annihilate what is good in us, what is godly, and do real damage in our world. This book might serve as a guide to help us recover the image of God in ourselves, and in so doing, help us make more visibly radiant the holiness of the world God has created for us to live in.

Kathleen Norris

Introduction

Listen to the teachings
and turn to them with the ear of your heart.
(*Rule of St. Benedict*)

God is our heart's desire. This book is intended for a person who is looking seriously for the right path on the spiritual journey. According to John Cassian, a fourth-century monk, three renunciations are required of us if we are on that journey. First, we must renounce our former way of life and move closer to our heart's desire, toward the interior life. Second, we must do the inner work (of asceticism) by renouncing our mindless thoughts. This renunciation is particularly difficult because we have little control over our thoughts. Third, and finally, we must renounce our own images of God so that we can enter into contemplation of God as God.

This book is about the second of those three renunciations: with thoughts, we grapple. Recurring themes or trains of thoughts run constantly through our consciousness. These thoughts—which can lead to desires and ultimately to passions—cluster in predictable ways: they are about food, sex, things, anger, dejection, acedia (or spiritual apathy), vainglory, and pride. Some are as familiar as breathing in and out. Some are starkly revealing, self-made obstacles which stand between us and our deepest desire.

In a contemporary world of complex spiritual teachings, which require sophisticated knowledge and difficult study, Cassian's lessons are very direct. He simply invited his early Christian readers to seek God by knowing and stabilizing their thoughts. More than 1600 years later, despite the insistent, chaotic hum of noise that surrounds us and occupies our minds, that same invitation is extended to us.

John Cassian was born in Dacia (present-day Romania) around the year 360 C.E. and traveled to Palestine and Egypt, where he spent twenty years as a monk, beginning his monastic life in a Greek-speaking *cenobium* (community of monks) in Bethlehem. Like many seekers of his time, inspired by the lives of the desert fathers and mothers of Egypt, he was not content merely to hear stories about those famous ascetics but went to meet them himself and remained there until 399. He was ordained in Constantinople by St. John Chrysotom in 405. In a wonderfully ingenious collection, he wrote down the teachings of thousands of solitaries of the early Christian era who lived in the deserts of Egypt, Syria, and Palestine. Finally, he took an excursion to Rome and Antioch and back to Bethlehem, which took him fifteen years. Toward the end of his life he founded two monasteries near Marseilles, in Southern Gaul, one for men and one for women. Cassian died around 435 and has a feast day celebrated on February 29 in the Orthodox Church. The Latin ordo (calendar of rituals) for 1997 has no listing of a day in honor of John Cassian.

For the purpose of his new monastic foundations, he wrote in Latin thirty-six books, twelve *Institutes* and twenty-four *Conferences* in the years 425–28. These works are edited to fit Cassian's system, yet are wonderfully instructive versions of the teachings and practices of the early desert fathers and mothers who showed by their lives that the spiritual journey, the search for God, requires the three renunciations just described.

The *Rule of St. Benedict* (RB), written one hundred years after the time of the desert fathers and mothers, was an extension of that same spirit. Benedict, in his short rule, refers seventy-eight times to Cassian's *Conferences* (*Conf.*) and sixty-eight times to the *Institutes* (*Inst.*). His dominant motif was the same then as it is today. Like Cassian, he invites his monks and nuns to make the three renunciations, to leave all and follow Christ, not by going to the desert as the fathers and mothers did, but by dwelling in a monastery. We say today that lay practitioners can also enter into the same transformative experience by being faithful to inner work. It is up to each person to decide what it takes to let go of a former way of life: to remain outwardly in the same environment, or to change his or her location or lifestyle. A change of exterior life for the sake of the interior life often happens at least once to some, many times to others. But no matter which environment is chosen, one must pay serious attention to the second renunciation: to let go of thoughts that are not toward prayer.

I have been prompted to write this book because, though there are many books on prayer, there is not much available for those of us working out this second difficult and important renunciation—where thoughts matter. In my work with the Monastic Interreligious Dialogue Board I have privileged conversation with Buddhist and Hindu practitioners. In listening to learned and wise Eastern teachers, I understand our culture's attraction to the East. The Christian counterpart to those teachings I find in the writings of the desert tradition of John Cassian. It is comforting to know that all the major religious traditions teach about the mind, that a serious seeker must undergo training to redirect the mind in order to follow a spiritual path.

To renounce one's thoughts may seem out-of-date to a casual observer—harsh, foreboding, even unrelenting. Yet the theory about this, developed over 2,000 years ago, is being rediscovered and reappropriated in our time by both mystics and scholars. A mind at peace, stilled, available for conscious thinking at will is of major value for those of us who confront chaos, confusion, noise, and numbness as we move into the third millennium.

Hopefully this book will help us reclaim the spirituality of the desert for our times so that we can integrate such teachings into our own contemporary lives. More importantly perhaps this book will enable serious seekers to name what they have already experienced. We can then devote our lives to discipleship.

A caution: The instructions regarding thoughts as presented by John Cassian constitute a system. To understand how thoughts and practices are linked, the reader needs to follow this presentation sequentially, chapter by chapter. The instructions here require us to enter into the mindset of wisdom from late antiquity. Renouncing our thoughts may seem very difficult and somewhat strange to minds accustomed to cultivating and expanding thoughts as a positive action. In the discussion here I have attempted to spell out my understanding of these ancient writings, but for your own study, you may want to refer to the primary literature listed in the bibliography. Finally, you may resist this middle renunciation as not right for you, not a direction in which you wish to go. Nonetheless, perhaps this little book will lead you to your next step, whatever it may be.

1. About Thoughts

If God is our heart's desire, then the heart knows its own path. All seekers somehow sense along the way the magnetism of the journey. However, through reflection on the teachings of the early desert hermits we can learn how the earliest Christians came to the mystical relationship with God that we, too, long for, not in the next life, but in this earthly one. The lives of the two hundred desert fathers and mothers that Cassian speaks about in his *Institutes* and *Conferences*[1] show clearly that it isn't enough to make a good resolution about one's intentions; deeds must follow.

However, it isn't that simple either. Deeds must be accompanied by right intentions. Serious seekers must train their minds to keep their goal ever before their consciousness. This interior work—this training of the mind—takes practice, a practice tradition calls the "ascetical life."

I remember when I first discovered that the primary work of the monastery wasn't apostolic service. It took me a few

---

1. John Cassian, *The Conferences*, Sulpitius Severus, Vincent of Lerins, John Cassian, *The Nicene, Post Nicene Fathers* 2.11, ed. Philip Schaff and Henry Wace, trans. Edgar C. S. Gibson (Grand Rapids, Mich.: Wm. B. Eerdmans Publishing Co., 1986; reprinted June 1991). (Contains all but *Institute VI* and *Conferences XII* and *XXII*.) The sections on sexuality were omitted in the Eerdmans edition. Unless otherwise stated, I used the *NPNF* series for all references except for the sections on the "Thought about Sex," where I used the Terrence Kardong translation: *Cassian on Chastity (Institute VI, Conference XII, Conference XXII)*. Introduction and trans. Terrence G. Kardong (Richardton, N.D.: Assumption Abbey Press, 1993).

years after final vows to understand that I wasn't called to the monastery simply to do ministry of teaching, nursing, or pastoral services. I discovered that the primary purpose of the Benedictine culture was to train one for the inner life. This ascetical life, this life of prayer, would naturally evolve into the fruit of hospitality and service.

The inner life, I would come to know, was my work and the work of the monastery. Only when I sensed the power of my thoughts and was able to renounce them could I hear the ever so small voice of God deep inside. And when I came to know God deep inside, I tasted something far greater than ordinary experience. Is this experience of knowing God deep within found only by monastics? Is this voice of God reserved only for a few or is this the same call to all seekers? No, there is a monk or a nun in every one of us, just as there is a desert hermit in every monastic. The work of every one of us is interior work, the practice of training our thoughts.

The desert tradition of early Christianity provides a common language to express a shared religious experience, and John Cassian's *Institutes* and *Conferences* provide an extremely clear description of practice in the Christian tradition, perhaps the clearest there is. The golden era lasted only two hundred years, from about 250 to 450 C.E., and during this time a spontaneous movement led people to the desert to live out a radical form of the Gospel: "To leave all and follow Christ." Immersed in the stillness of the harsh desert, intending to totally renounce the world by dwelling alone, these hermits experienced first, however, only raw emotions.[2]

In the old, often retold, mythical tale of Abba Anthony, we hear him tell about the vicissitudes of renouncing wealth,

---

2. Douglas Burton-Christie, *The Word in the Desert* (New York: Oxford Press, 1993), 73ff.

honor, status, relationships, and comfort, only to find that the thoughts of wealth, honor, status, relationships, and comfort had followed him into his solitude. Rather than moving into a mystical experience with God, his mind kept his previous life before him. Prayer was very difficult because, although he was in the desert, his mind was back home.

He had a second renunciation to undergo. He realized that his thoughts mattered and that they had to be taken seriously, because if he did not take them seriously, he could not pray. He began to train himself to notice his thoughts, laying them out, rather than resisting them. This holy father of monasticism then learned to redirect his thoughts, either by rethinking them or by placing a prayer alongside the thought.

Thinkers many years before Anthony had discovered that there were clusters of themes that recurred over and over in the silence of their hearts: thoughts about food, sex, things, anger, dejection, acedia, vainglory, and pride. The wrestling with these thoughts they considered the negative part of the practice of controlling them; the alternate, positive action was to fill their minds with inspired and traditional prayers. Cassian used the term *lectio* and Benedict used both *lectio* and *lectio divina* to recommend the practice of this traditional form of prayer for Christians. This particular method of sacred reading provided a way to listen to the Scriptures with the ear of one's heart.

We need to reclaim that tradition that served the desert fathers and mothers so well. They literally entered into the text that revealed God to them. The wisdom of a later tradition, made popular by St. Hugh, taught that this *lectio divina* has three books: the book of nature, the book of experience, and the book of Scripture.[3]

---

3. Bernard McGinn, *The Growth of Mysticism* (New York: Crossroad, 1994), 386.

When you do *lectio divina* with Scripture it has these stages: The first is *lectio*, reading, to study and understand the literal sense of the text. For the first few centuries of the Christian era, Scripture was the prevailing prism for the wisdom of the culture. There was no split of the secular from the sacred as we have today. It is important to understand Scripture because that revelatory text mediates faith handed on from one generation to the next.

To study the literal meaning of Scripture, we need to do five things: First, note the genre, the kind of literature it is. Second, study the author(s) and see what the overall purpose of the work is intended to convey. Third, read the passage and examine the text with any footnotes, seeing the context of the passage, how it is framed in the sequence of the text, what goes before and after the selected text. Fourth, study the references to see if they refer to other similar texts, and look up those references that attract us. Fifth, look at the subtle differences and nuances of the meaning, checking several translations, if necessary, to see how the meaning is changed through the translation.

All five of these simple aids for reading Scripture are available for our use in a variety of Bibles in any bookstore. More advanced students can do deeper study or exegesis on the passage, read commentaries, study parallel texts, or contrast translations in different languages. This simple, five-tool approach, however, is designed to grasp the meaning, yet not get lost in an inexhaustible search for scholarship. The *lectio* in *lectio divina* is meant to be reading for prayer, not for teaching, preaching, or writing.

The second stage in *lectio divina* is *meditatio*, thinking and reflecting on the meaning of the text in order to understand its significance. The hermits used the time in their cells (individual sleeping/study spaces) to immerse themselves in the word of God until it became natural to them, a prayer coming from within as well as without. Today we, too, can memorize or internalize the text by reading it over and over, by writing journals, by engaging in artistic expressions of the meaning through music, dance, or art. Helpful starting places to begin the process of *meditatio* are the Psalms or the Gospels.

The third stage, *oratio*, is living into the text by putting it into your life either in prayer, work, or acts of love. The Scripture is no longer simply about God but addresses God in words of ardor, gratitude, and praise. Scripture becomes the language of a loving friendship. The solitaries chanted psalms and prayed as continuously as they could. We can pray the Jesus Prayer or keep company with Christ in our hearts through dialogue. What I notice, living with nuns as I do, is that work becomes for them a conscious prayer, each action done mindfully in the presence of God. There's a natural inclination to practice the presence of God through mindfulness, short prayers, explicit acts of charity, and acts of self-sacrifice.

Finally *contemplatio* means sitting in silence with no thoughts, the unspeakable joy of simply resting in God, the classic definition of contemplation, according to Gregory the Great. All sacred texts have this as their end and design. What is important about *lectio divina* for us today is to see that, unlike the desert fathers and mothers who went through various stages of enlightenment, we don't have to go to the desert to let go of our thoughts and to learn to pray we can do this prayer form in our own dwellings. *Lectio divina* is a personal or domestic prayer form. The fruit of *lectio divina* is a conscious, living, and active relationship with God.

Newcomers or travelers who heard of the desert fathers and mothers went out to the desert and asked how they too could establish a mystical relationship with God. In this, the earliest form of spiritual direction, the amma or abba who had already experienced God and had been through the middle renunciation of thoughts was able to see into the hearts and thoughts of the seeker. She or he would give that seeker a word, a "saying," or a story that would help the hearer move toward his or her own salvation. Such a transmission was based on an honest exchange between an enlightened teacher and a disciple who was ready not only to hear the word, but also to do the word. Many of these more than two thousand sayings are about the eight thoughts. Cassian, using many of these sayings, wrote conferences or long discourses for novice monastics. But before we examine those actual teachings, we need to have an understanding of how to talk about the body, mind, and soul and of how thoughts, desires, and passions emerge.

In late antiquity Christian thought was influenced by Neoplatonic and Stoic thinkers. Christians baptized Plato's philosophy. While Platonic thought seems otherworldly in its synthesis, ideals, and goals, actually Greek thinking is very down to earth. Experience is considered the basis of self-reflection. Neoplatonists had a sophisticated understanding about the chatter in one's inner life. Today we have moved past Greek thinking and prefer more immediacy toward God without a philosophical system, but we can learn much from the best of the Hellenistic tradition that shaped much of our history. Early desert fathers and mothers of the third to fifth centuries noticed that thoughts and awareness of thoughts were the key to insight into the body, mind, and soul.

The body was considered a vehicle for the soul. The mind enlivens the body and gives it the ability to be reflective about its own being. When the mind leaves the body, the body is dead. The soul enlivens the body and the mind and unites the body–mind into a person that transcends time and space. The soul, which will live beyond the lifespan of the body and the mind, is the ideal state for experiencing happiness. During earthly life, although the body and the mind are afflicted with limitations, the soul is not. However, the soul can be diminished if the free will of the person makes poor choices.

In making use of this body, mind, and soul paradigm, the Christian desert wisdom said that the Holy Spirit is the soul of the soul that enlivens the total human person. This divinization is total, pervasive, and operative if the obstacles due to original sin are removed. The major obstacle is sin, or turning away from our Creator who made us to be in the likeness of God. Sin is the end stage of wrong thoughts, desires, and passions. Sin promotes a vicious life of evil. We can reverse this tendency by using our thoughts, desires, and passions for good. This is a virtuous life of grace.

Today we resist dualist models that make simplistic assumptions by contrasting opposites. We consider it dangerous to judge some things good and some things bad when most reality is a mixture of good and bad and it's not certain that the bad isn't really a benefit and the good an illusion. Most postmodern believers embrace a spirituality that is charged with the cosmic divinization that Pierre Teilhard de Chardin made so attractive.[4] Many of us can no longer see salvation as a private affair between the soul and God. We are social beings striving for a universal conscience that espouses the *all* of us in each *one* of us. However, we cannot get to that cosmic dimension without training of the mind. The desert wisdom had a sense of the unity of all persons and the impact of each of our thoughts upon that unity. Furthermore, the ammas and the abbas gave us practical insights and simple teachings about how thoughts function.

Thoughts, these teachers said, rise in the mind. They come in a sequence, a train of thoughts. We are not our thoughts. Thoughts come and thoughts go. Unaccompanied thoughts pass quickly.

---

4. Ewert Cousins, *Christ of the 21st Century* (New York: Continuum, 1992), 50–52.

Thoughts that are thought about become desires. Desires that are thought about become passions. Good thoughts become virtues. Bad thoughts become bad desires; bad passions or habits of action become sins. The passions are acted upon us when we consent, then the passions move from passive to active engagement.

We can redirect our thoughts. We can notice our thoughts at the first instance and can get control of our mind. A mind in control of itself is at peace.

First thoughts beget second thoughts, which become intentions. Intentions constitute motivations and indicate where the heart resides. Motivation moves the will to decide and act on the thought. Decisions give voice to the choices we intend to act upon.

Attention to our thoughts reveals our intentions. Right deeds must be accompanied by the right reason, or the deed becomes wrong for us in that particular situation. Discernment is our ability to do the right deed with the right intention or motivation.

The thoughts that we find in our interior chatter cluster into eight themes which recur constantly. These eight thoughts are manifested to the self in solitude because our exterior life follows us into the private chambers of our heart. These thoughts are classic since they recur in every person of every era and cycle continuously.

In the desert literature the training of a novice first focuses on external concerns such as what to eat, what to wear, what to do all day long, and how to live in the desert environment. The second set of instructions are about how to deal with the eight thoughts: about food, about sex, about things, about anger, about dejection, about acedia, about vainglory, and about pride. The order of these thoughts make a difference, because they move in a sequence from simple to complex. These teachings reveal that while our life choices govern what we wear, eat, and do with our time all day, all persons, no matter what their way of life, are subject to the eight thoughts. We make choices about our food and drink, about how we express ourselves sexually, and about how to get things that we need. None of us has had a week without angry feelings and thoughts of dejection and elation. We become weary and tired of the spiritual struggle at moments, perhaps even for years. And finally, who of us has not felt the surge of pride that is pervasively behind every one of our accomplishments and underneath our every failure?

When we think of the eight thoughts, we are immediately reminded of the seven capital sins. Gregory the Great was the first one to list the "eight thoughts" as "seven capital sins." (Vainglory was usually deleted and, if treated at all, it was under the label of pride.) Though this terminology of capital sins found its way into every catechism, the impact of the thinking, which generates our acting, was sometimes ignored. The emphasis on sin, which this change in terminology effected, tended to distort the earlier emphasis on the richness of the interior life of a serious seeker who, by striving toward purity of heart, longs intensely for a significant relationship with God.

This relationship requires of us three renunciations: First, we must renounce our former way of life. We follow our calling or accept our chosen "vocation." Notice the language: we accept our *chosen vocation*. The choice is not to become a practitioner, but to accept the invitation calling us to this awesome way of life. We didn't create it for ourselves. We are responding to a longing embedded deep in our hearts.

In the early desert tradition this renunciation was of family, profession, wealth, status, and children. The seeker went to the desert to pray, creating the earliest form of what we now call "religious life." Today seekers renounce their former way of life through many choices. Some choose to join a religious community or go to a seminary. Some renounce their former way of life of being single, of owning property, of following a particular profession, or of being socially prominent.

I've seen both nuns and lay seekers become serious enough about their interior practice to rearrange their schedule or make a special space for prayer in their bedrooms, houses, or apartments. I've seen them begin to stop at a sacred shrine or chapel on a daily basis; change previous interests, relationships, hobbies, and patterns in order to take up a serious meditation practice that requires time, silence, and solitude. It seems that the first step to an ongoing practice is this first renunciation, the renunciation of our former way of life. Even though the work is interior, we mortals require space and time to attend to the heart and training of the mind.

Many try to avoid this renunciation of their former way of life by trying to live two or three parallel lives. A nun in a convent, for instance, may try to keep up all of her former relationships, especially family obligations, or a lay seeker may keep up a life of travel that precludes any spiritual practices. The serious seeker, on the other hand, gives up her former way of life because she or he realizes that the single-minded pursuit of the spiritual life takes total energy. One forsakes earlier patterns. One exercises control to keep one's eyes on the new goals. One seems to have a natural inclination and eagerness for the new way of life. One is like a person in love. It isn't as hard to leave home when another passion draws you to your beloved. His or her voice is persistent and utterly alluring. It whispers softly, inviting to intimate conversation, friendship, reading, art, music. God the lover is real and forgetfulness is not an option.

This first renunciation may be described in many ways: flight from the world, conversion of lifestyle, change of heart, repentance, *xeniteia* (flight from humankind, which in desert times resulted in entering the monastery or becoming a hermit). This flight, rather than an attempt to escape from someone or something, is rather for the sake of knowing oneself by knowing one's thoughts. To know our thoughts is an essential step in redirecting our heart to God in prayer. And whether flight is to monastery or desert cave, the key practice leading us to know our thoughts, and to renounce our thoughts, is silence. Wisdom tells us that silence will teach us everything.

A certain brother went to Abbot Moses in Scete and asked him for a good word. And the elder said to him, "Go, sit in your cell, and your cell will teach you everything." The Evangelist says that the kingdom of God comes not with observation, nor here and there, but within you. But nothing else can be within you (*Conf.* I.12).

However, to get to the place of silence, the serious seeker must make that first renunciation: his former way of living, her exterior life. Our exterior life must be ordered for the work of the soul. At the most elementary level, silence allows us to know ourselves, because we move against the automatic chatter of unconscious living.

The second renunciation requires us not only to renounce our thoughts, but also to renounce our attachment to our thoughts. If I take up a new exterior environment and still retain all the thoughts of my former way of life, then I, as a seeker, am not present to my vocation. I miss the benefits of the commitment to religious life or to a marriage. In the cell I must learn the silence that becomes perfect stillness, that allows me to renounce the tyranny of thoughts.

As I said earlier, the theory about thoughts postulates that there is a systematic order to our thoughts, from food through sex, things, anger, dejection, acedia, vainglory, and pride. But psychologically, in practice, each of us must keep in mind Abbot Serapion's teaching (*Conf.* V.27) that we must know that our battles are not all fought in the same order, because the attacks are not always made on us in the same way. Each one of us ought to battle against the thought that vexes us whether it's first or third or eighth on the list. We must see what's in our eyes, as in a mirror, and start there.

Did the early monks rise above their passions? According to Thomas Merton, it seems that the praise of monks as "beyond all passion" came from tourists who passed briefly through the deserts and went home to write books about what they had seen, rather than from those who had spent their whole life in the wilderness.[5] The monks themselves used this very struggle as the path. However, it does seem that a state of quiet did emerge for many of them. The goal was prayer, not freedom from the work it takes to pray.

The third renunciation—after renouncing one's former way of life and then renouncing one's thoughts—is more difficult than either of the previous ones. It is to renounce our very idea of God. Since God is beyond all images, thoughts, and concepts, then we must renounce our cherished beliefs for the sake of loving God as God. This third renunciation is a natural fruit of years and years of prayer and meditation and/or is God's gift. If we persist in the spiritual life we experience dark times of doubt and nothingness as we are weaned from an immature self-made piety. Through *lectio divina* we move naturally from image to image and finally become "at home" in imageless prayer, pure prayer.[6] St. Anthony said that the prayer of the monk is not perfect until he no longer realizes the fact that he is praying (*Conf.* IX.31).

This deepest form of prayer, contemplation, is described as a fire that burns without consuming, drawing the soul into total absorption into God. It is celebrated and described in the rich literature of the desert tradition of which John

---

5. Thomas Merton, *The Wisdom of the Desert* (New York: New Directions, 1960), 30.
6. Ibid., 8.

Cassian's *Institutes* and *Conferences* form only a portion. His catechesis on prayer is so outstanding that his sections on the thoughts are overshadowed. Perhaps that is another reason why little attention has been paid to the middle renunciation, the renunciation of thoughts.

Pure prayer is beyond thoughts. All thoughts are renounced. Peace prevails, *apatheia* (passionlessness) floods the soul and the mind is profoundly stilled. Mystery!

As we become detached from the ego we shed the biases of our culture and we move toward pure prayer. Ego is the voice of the self. The I-thought is ego. We cannot proceed from step one, leaving our former way of life, and jump into pure prayer without this middle asceticism (practice) of relinquishing thoughts. We must seek God and not our own thoughts. If we have not renounced our thoughts, it is easy to think that our thoughts are God. God is both beyond our grasping—not our next thought after this one—and also not a thought at all! It is very difficult to undergo the first two renunciations, to let go of our former way of life, and also to let go of our interior thoughts, but these are only steps, and necessary ones, for the deepest conversion toward God as God and the experience of pure prayer (contemplation).

In this book, we will see what John Cassian advises us about the second renunciation: We will take each of the eight classic thoughts and study the teachings for this early Christian tradition. Thoughts, he says, matter. The first thought that matters most for beginners is the one "about food." Why shouldn't that universal experience of food be the mother of all teachings in the spiritual life?

2. About Food

The first of the eight thoughts treated by John Cassian is thinking about food. The impulse to eat and drink is natural and instinctual. At its first inkling, however, food is simply a thought "I would like a cup of tea." The thought *happens* to be about food or drink.

As stated earlier, the earliest training for a novice in the spiritual life is to notice that we have thoughts, and the major reason the work of the spiritual journey is so difficult is because we seldom notice these thoughts. Thoughts are part of our internal world, and the spiritual journey involves interior work because interior work governs our external life. We generally live life in a cloud of unthinking, totally unaware of the inner stirrings and sensitivities of our hearts.

Fasting is a good practice to adopt as we start serious work in the spiritual life. Most people think of fasting as eating nothing for long periods of time. However, John Cassian's teaching on fasting is that we should simply put food and our thoughts about food into proper balance, eating only at meals and not in between. If we fast in this way, we can get in touch with our thoughts, because when we feel the bodily need of food and drink, we begin to notice our *thoughts* about food and we know we must let them go without acting on them if we hope to progress in calming our mind. If all we think about are bodily needs, then conscious prayer remains a distant goal. If we can't tame the thought of food, there is no hope of getting control of the more difficult thoughts, such as sex and anger.

First I have an image of food; then that image leads to a desire to eat it. A passion rises to the surface to do whatever it takes to get that food or drink. Hunger rises with a double force. It's now 11:35 in the morning and I feel a sinking hunger. I had coffee, juice, and toast at 6:00 A.M. Now I would like to go to the kitchen before lunch and have a glass of milk. Perhaps I should just get a refrigerator for my room. This train of thoughts (*logismois*) trails on from one desire to another, and the cycle repeats itself over and over again. It can be an obsession that distances me from God, others, and myself.

Creation's original condition, as it was described in the myth of the Garden of Eden in the Book of Genesis, was well ordered. Human beings, in a state of innocence, enjoyed the unmediated presence of God. This story of Adam and Eve illustrates, however, the tendencies we have to destroy this innocence, to move away from God, to engage in evil thoughts and activities. The teachings on food help show us how to use our habits of eating and drinking to be of service to our search for God, thereby helping to restore the original order in the universe through the spiritual life of contemplation.

The first teaching about food is to notice my thoughts and the train of thoughts they inspire. "Food-thoughts" will become conscious to me as I try to follow John Cassian's straightforward and healthy teachings about food and drink: Refrain from eating too much, but also refrain from eating too little. Eat at the designated time. Refrain from eating before or after meals. Eat the type of food appropriate to the season and the geographic region in which I live. My menu should not be too rarefied or delicate, nor should I select foods that are inadequate for the body's sustenance. I should prefer a middle fare.

When food becomes my dominant thought, it becomes the center of my interior life. The self talking to the self becomes a conversation about my desire for food or drink. Using these guidelines of Cassian, a right ordering of my desire for food and drink removes the constant deliberation about what to eat, when, and how much. I am out of balance when I shift too far in any one direction. "Excesses meet," say the ancients (*Conf.* II.16). Eating too little or eating too much are equally harmful. Extremes are indicators of thoughts being out of control. This first thought, the thought about food, helps the practitioner understand about balance in eating and drinking. If I can eat and drink moderately then I can be moderate in other thoughts as well, thoughts like sex, things, and anger.

Control of my thoughts, desires, and passions is for the sake of single-minded thinking about God. With fewer thoughts dominating my consciousness I will eventually experience God's interior communication with me. Again, the content of the first of the eight thoughts, food, is not so much about food as it is about the practice of using the food thought as a training tool. As we will see with the other seven thoughts, what the thought is does not matter; what matters is how I redirect my thoughts to God. The practice is to surrender my own thoughts, to listen to the thought (eventually the Word) of God. This renunciation is the first stage in learning to pray: to lift up my thoughts and mind to God.

The value of moderation is that extremes do not become another thought and eventually more intrusive than the original thought of food. If I am a compulsive eater, I have no thought in my consciousness other than food. This compulsive thinking leads to compulsive action. There is no distance between the thought, the desire, and the action. This is reversed by fasting. My thinking patterns are checked by my fasting practice, that is, eating at the appointed time, eating what is served and not desiring an inappropriate quality of food.

How do I know when the appointed time is, and how do I know what the moderate quantity of food and drink and appropriate quality of nourishment are? To discern such things is to practice the virtuous life.

To discern is to sort out my thoughts, one at a time. Is

this the right time to eat or to drink? How much is enough? Do I need the best quality of food? What would be healthy for me? Such discerning in the presence of God leads to fasting that eventually provides great benefits for me in a spiritually wholesome life.

Thoughts rise unsolicited from my unconscious and come in from the external stimuli of my exterior world, clamoring for attention. My heart desires to make choices. Discernment is the art of learning how to make right choices that are appropriate for myself at a particular time, place, and stage of my life. After a few years of conscious discernment, the body begins to establish a preference for a well-ordered pattern of eating and it actually becomes natural and even easy. The urges diminish in strength and frequency and equanimity follows. Peace is possible!

We do not loath food, nor do we have guilt or shame about eating and drinking. Food takes its proper place, often becoming an opportunity for feasting and celebrating with others. A solitary cup of morning coffee takes on sacramental dimensions in the dawn. First light is a precious time for contemplatives. Thoughts are slow, deliberate, reflective, and close to the heart. As with other values of the spiritual life, the single one-thought-at-a-time experience becomes more pleasurable with more practice. When the mind is stilled the smell, taste, and feel of that first cup of coffee is special and enjoyed as if for the first time!

Through an awakened power of consciousness, I practice being aware rather than being asleep and unconscious. This is not a practice of being aware of the self for the sake of the self. It is a practice of being aware of the self for the sake of another. The self in service of the other is like an act of worship, fundamentally more important than a self absorbed by self, grasping to feed an insatiable thirst.

Food connects us with the chain of life. All life forms

nourish and need to be nourished. The "original order" of things is friendly, natural, organic, relational, whole, and simple. Eating properly balances energies. Work and rest, play and leisure become harmonious. According to the desert tradition, in order that fasting stay pure, any excess food is given to the poor. To be always mindful of the poor keeps a check on my intentions. A well-ordered lifestyle of work and prayer is usually economically successful, but the "worldly" benefits must never be in service of the ego. Therefore, the poor actually serve us because they mediate Christ for us.

Gluttony is the pattern of eating indiscriminately with no thought of how this food is feeding my spiritual life. Eating and drinking can be unreflective and even gross. The spiritual practice of eating right is mindful and deliberate. We connect with the rest of life and live with all God's creatures.

Rather than seeing my meals as an episodic austerity, when I keep only the prescribed days of fast and abstinence, moderate fasting becomes a lifestyle. If I have an abiding consciousness of Christ in the center of my life, my need for food takes on right order. There is proportion. Everyone has enough.

The first struggle with food and drink is a wonderful place for beginners to start, even though we are all beginners; it takes a lifetime to develop disciplines into a patterned lifestyle. The lessening of the grip of the thought of food and of drink eventually provides the opportunity for other levels of consciousness to emerge. This is why food and drink addictions are so harmful to the interior life. The seeker learns to resist thoughts, desires, and passions that return only to the self. The goal is to love God and be for others.

The stories in the desert tradition are full of disregard for our own needs, for the sake of hospitality. Sometimes we are told to eat more than we want in order to accompany another, or we might be required to eat less depending on the circumstances. The rule of charity governs the willingness to be detached from our own preferences about which to eat, how much, and the quality of food we take.

It is surprising to learn how late in antiquity St. Anthony and the desert monastics discovered the link between fasting and meditation. Together these practices dismantle compulsions. Practitioners lose the inclination to excess. Enough is enough.

Once we get our own lives in order, the tendency is to then judge another's correct amount of food and drink. To judge another's portion is not for me to decide. All practices are to be guided by discretion and for each of us there are differing requirements depending on our age, health, and work load. How much is enough for someone else is not for me to judge. The practice of the devout is not to judge another but to practice for myself a balanced way of eating and drinking according to the graces given me along the way. When I learn discretion as a virtue, I know the factors involved in my decisions, it is apparent that no one can know all those variables for another. Discernment is personal, an individual practice of self-judgment. To misuse this freedom is a fundamental temptation of prejudice. Each of us needs to judge only ourself and not another. Abbot Theodore gives these words to his disciples: "Youll be judged as you judge. Its dangerous to act like you are God, the Judge. You don't know why they are doing what they are doing. They might be pardoned, but we will have sinned" (*Inst.* V.30). The monastic can't make any progress in chastity (or any of the virtues) if he or she continues to jude others harshly (*Conf.* XII.16).

In the section about food John Cassian continues sharing the wisdom of Abbot Theodore:

> We knew also Abbot Theodore, a man gifted with the utmost holiness and with perfect knowledge not only in practical life, but also in understanding the Scriptures, which he had not acquired so much by study and reading, or worldly education,

as by purity of heart alone: since he could with difficulty understand and speak but a very few words of the Greek language.
This man when he was seeking an explanation of some most
difficult question, continued without ceasing for seven days and
nights in prayer until he discovered by a revelation from the
Lord the solution of the question propounded. (*Inst.* V.33)

When some of the brethren were wondering at the
splendid light of his knowledge and were asking of Theodore
some meanings of Scripture, he said that a monk who wanted
to acquire a knowledge of the Scriptures ought not to spend
his labor on the works of commentators, but rather keep all
the efforts of his mind and intentions of his heart set on puri-
fying himself from vices. When these are driven out, at once
the eye of the heart, as if the veil of the passions were
removed, will begin, as it were, naturally to gaze on the mys-
teries of Scripture: since they were not declared to us by the
grace of the Holy Spirit in order that they should remain
unknown and obscure (*Inst.* V.34).

When I fast I take the first step toward discernment.
Fasting leads to moderation and I begin to be able to sort and
control my thoughts. The more I control them, the better able
I am to discern right actions. As a result, with a greater purity of heart, I am better able to see into the Scriptures and
understand better their dynamic meanings.

Are there teachings about the wrong foods?

Early Christians tried to move from the letter of the law
to the intent of the law regarding purification of the mind,
heart, and body. The Trappist Charles Cummings gathered
together the Christian references from Scripture and *The Rule
of Benedict* (RB) regarding food.[1]

---

1. Charles Cummings, *Monastic Practices* (Kalamazoo, Mich.:
Cistercian Publications, 1986), 123–24.

Jesus fasted in the desert (Mt 1:2) and also ate and drank in public (Mt 11:18–19). St. Benedict called for fasting from "the flesh of four-footed animals" (*RB* 39); exceptions were made for the weak and sick. Wine was reluctantly permitted, but limited in Benedict's rule (*RB* 40:3).

The earliest teachings report that in Scripture meat was not food for humans (Gn 1:29–30) because all animals, including human beings, were vegetarians and lived harmoniously together in a peaceful kingdom (Is 11:69); but after the Fall and the Flood, God explicitly permitted the consumption of meat (Gn 9:3). Also in the New Testament there is stress on freedom in the new covenant: we know that "all foods are clean" (Rom 14:20) and that the "kingdom of God is not a matter of eating or drinking, but of justice, peace, and the joy that is given by the Holy Spirit" (Rom 14:17). If our practice of vegetarianism is found to be healthier, more symbolic, or less expensive than eating meat, these are not benefits that necessarily bring us closer to God. St. Paul says, in a discussion of eating meat sacrificed to idols and later sold at market, "We suffer no loss through failing to eat, and we gain no favor by eating" (1 Cor 8:8).

Cummings recommends that instead of playing off the value of one practice against the other we should follow St. Paul's directive. He grounded both practices, the eating of meat and the not eating of meat, in the radical Christian obligation to honor God and avoid offending the conscience of others (1 Cor 8:13; Rom 14:20). He says that the Benedictine motive for partial or total vegetarianism is found in the Benedictine principle of glorifying God in all things (*RB* 57; 1 Pt 4:11). "The one who eats does so to honor the Lord, and he gives thanks to God. The one who does not eat abstains to honor the Lord, and he too gives thanks to God" (Rom 14:6).

I believe we need to practice our own implementation of the spirit of the law, keeping in mind others' needs as well as ours. Scientific evidence is mounting as to the quantity, quality, and source of nutrients each of us needs, and resources needed to be shared by all of us living on this planet. A proportionate distribution of earth's resources will become a spiritual value when each of us takes seriously the needs of the other. However, we must not judge others' interpretations of the spirit of the law; discernment governs each one's practice.

Are there no foods that should be eliminated from the diet of a serious seeker?

I asked the ninety-year-old sisters I live with what their earliest memories of the customs about foods, fasting, and feasting were. Their stories showed that food was scarce and meals were the produce of the farm, similar to the local fare of other German immigrants in Southern Indiana. The discipline was to surrender their will and be willing to eat what was served, at the appointed time. When they were young nuns, severe fasting was discouraged and individual permission was required from the superior. Obedience and humility prevailed regarding food. Before Vatican II the fast before Holy Communion and the abstinence from meat on Friday were very strictly observed, but the spirit behind the law became obscured by history. When the law was lifted the practice vanished. The wholistic revolution has replaced asceticism in postmodern lifestyles. Fasting was supplanted by dieting.

Now when fasting is done in my monastery, the individual is responsible for its observance. Most nuns I know try to observe a purification fast on their monthly desert day, when they dedicate a day to silence and prayer. On all other days the three moderations are practiced through the common life: to eat at the right time, to eat "enough," to eat what is served. To participate in feasts is expected, too. Both food preparation and celebration call for more dedication. To stay at the common table is a particular discipline. Hospitality is both the fruit and the thorn ever beckoning us beyond our own agenda. The older sisters consistently demonstrate that poise of everydayness being ready to meet, greet, and enjoy the daily bread.

Daily meditators often lose much of their appetite for meat, getting their energy from lighter foods lower on the food chain, indicating a relationship between being a vegetarian and being a serious meditator. The contemplative life thrives on less complex food as well as single-mindedness in thought. A higher quality of well-being for the inner work seems to prevail when we are not doing heavy-duty digestion!

In the Hindu tradition, one must qualify for the practice of meditation. False quiet can be simple indolence. Part of the training to learn how to meditate is to refrain from foods such as meat, alcohol, vegetables like garlic, radishes, and onions. These foods are considered to be intrinsically harmful to the interior life. My Hindu friends are especially aware of vibrations that must be stilled before the meditation. If you eat the flesh of animals that have been killed by violence, those vibrations affect the foods that you ingest. A meditator also ought to be attentive to the person who cooks and serves the food, because that person's attitude enters into the food. Hindus talk about being willing to move out the lethargic energies that are connected with the lower passions and exchange them for higher spiritual energies.[2] They do this by sacrifice. In their tradition, an authentic guru who has been given the power of revealing truth, can simply look at an individual and know what is needed for his or her energies.

Eastern Christians were forbidden all animal food during Lent; not only meat and fish but eggs (as coming from the hen),

2. Mary Margaret Funk, interview with Swami Harshananda of Bangalore, *Bulletin of Monastic Interreligious Dialogue* 57 (1997): 10.

milk (as coming from the cow), and all milk produce. Thus—with the one exception of honey—Lenten food is limited to vegetables, cereals, fungi, and vegetable oils. In the nineteenth century fasting was still strictly observed by Orthodox Russians.[3]

Perhaps as a Christian I must surrender my willfulness in order to enter into a willingness to eat what is given, at the appointed time and in the appropriate location and season. Fasting helps me know my thoughts and keeps me supple enough to hear the grace moving through my heart. Food should not dominate my consciousness; it is only a tool for my relationship with God. But on the other hand food should not be a barrier to keep me from deeper stillness and a predisposition toward prayer. A fruit of the contemplative life is the joy of eating mindfully with gratitude.

The second thought is "about sex." Our most intimate urges confront us in the spiritual life!

---

3.   Macarius, Starets of Optino, *Russian Letters of Direction 1834–1860*, ed., trans., and foreword by Iulia De Beausobre (Westminster: Dacre Press, 1944; reprinted by Robert Maclehouse and Co., Glasgow: The University Press, 1947), 47

3. About Sex

The second thought, about sex, is generally not about a beloved's qualities but about the physical or emotional needs he or she represents. This desire can lead to lust. The teaching about sex follows and is modeled on the teaching about food because the disciplines of fasting and silence which control the tendency to gluttony also provide a method to redirect and diminish the seductive thought of sex.

Sex is so powerful that the tradition often advises an indirect means for taming this passion rather than directly confronting it. Usually a direct approach is fruitless because so much of the sex drive lies beneath consciousness. Cassian recommends fasting and prayer as means for diminishing sex urges. Other indirect means are engaging in physical exercise, maintaining distance from the person who is the object of the passion, and working with dreams rather than working through ordinary consciousness.

The demands that sex makes on us produce a lifetime of struggle, even for the highest saints. Rare are reports about those who are given the total gift of equanimity regarding sexual thoughts. Although through God's grace passions will subside and the mind will return to stillness, the desert tradition nonetheless describes a person's struggle for equanimity as initially very difficult. At first the practitioner is "in training" and needs the letter and spirit of the law to form his conscience. Sometimes it takes a few weeks or a few years, but once God grants the gift of freedom from those struggles, a period of calm sets in, and the fruit of chastity is felt. The chaste one is naked before the Creator God and belongs wholly to the

Beloved. Is chastity attainable for us today? or does this teaching belong to a bygone era?

Let us turn to the teachings regarding sex found in John Cassian's *Institutes* and *Conferences*. These teachings of his are somewhat difficult to retrieve, having been given to celibate monastics in the desert centuries ago. Cassian was writing only for monastics, so how could the teachings about the thought of sex be relevent to lay seekers as well? Terrence Kardong, O.S.B., and Columba Stewart, O.S.B., cautioned me that Cassian's teachings pertained to those who had already accepted the monastic promises. Yet it seems to me that if the other seven thoughts could be helpful teachings for lay persons, then sex should also somehow be of benefit.

When I was in India and engaged in Hindu dialogue with householders and monastics, I learned the holistic way of moving toward holiness through the stages of renunciation deeply imbedded in their ancient culture. These phases are not to be done in the series of lifetimes of those who believe in reincarnation, but are directives for all who want to achieve God-Realization or Enlightenment in this lifetime. The four stages of Indo-Aryan life are first the student, second the householder, third the retired person or hermit, and fourth the monk or ascetic. In each of these stages the goal is to move toward celibacy as a conscious effort. Certain persons choose to become a monastic for the whole of their lives, but all, married or monastic, are called to renounce this world and move toward the spiritual world. In other words, everyone is celibate at some point, whether he or she is monastic or married. The practice comes at a different phase in one's life for different persons.

The Asian religions use the word *celibacy* to describe this practice of renunciation during three of the four phases of one's life: (a) as a student, (b) as a retired person or hermit, and (c) as a monastic or ascetic. Sexual engagement is proper and expected during the second phase of one's life, e.g., being a householder. According to one source:

> The sages had phenomenal memory acquired through the practice of celibacy. Celibacy is no other than conservation of energy. The sages of ancient India knew that a person who did not waste his energy through unrestrained sensual pursuits, particularly sexual activity, could greatly enhance his memory and other mental faculties. (*Patanjala Yogasutra*, Sadhanapada, Aphorism 38: "By the establishment of continence energy is gained.") The other benefits of celibacy were greater longevity and *dharma shakti*—the ability to understand the deeper meaning of the Scriptures. Equipped with such memory the sages were able to memorize the numerous Vedic Truths. Their students, who were also celibate, heard these Truths, memorized them, and shaped their lives accordingly. As they were learned by hearing and not by reading, the Truths came to be known as Shruti, which literally means hearing.[1]

The use of the word *celibate* conveys this notion that married persons are celibate toward all others except their mates and that before and after the householder phase there is a choice to move one's life and lifestyle toward transcending sexual consciousness for the sake of the spiritual life. One attains the total celibate lifestyle only after sexual goals have been fulfilled. Sex in this view is in service of a higher life beyond this one. Celibacy is also taught as a practice for enhancing meditation wherein one's subtle, spiritual energies rise because of the sublimating effect. There is no antisexual attitude, nor is one asexual, but sex is a conscious stage to move through. A good marriage is one where these goals are

1. Swami Bhaskaranda, *The Essentials of Hinduism* (Seattle, Wash.: Viveka Press, The Vedanta Society of Western Washington), 11.

achieved mutually and with concerted effort to do the most loving thing for the relationship to each other.

There is a misconception that Tantric practices of Buddhism use the sexual energies in a normal manner of copulation to raise the subtle energies (Unexcelled Yoga tantras). When and if this is done, according to H. H. the Dalai Lama, there is such high training that the male when aroused emits no semen. In dialogue with Monastic Interreligious Dialogue Board, he recommended total refraining from these Tantric practices for our age since the proper training is not available.

To avoid confusion from now on, I'll use the term *married* for householders and *celibate* for monastics. For both groups the goal is to transcend sex consciousness. This includes transcending gender consciousness, which will be beneficial in the third renunciation when one renounces his or her image of God.

John Cassian begins by noting that thoughts of another person's body rise first in the imagination. Sometimes these thoughts come from a past experience, a recent contact, a chance image, or hearing about someone else's encounter with a sexually attractive person. It is natural to have sexual fantasies. Male nocturnal emissions occur, he says, as often as once in four months (*Conf.* XXII.23) or once every two months (*Inst.* VI.20). He talks frankly about dreams that occur and recur and move one to sexual arousal (*Conf.* XII.7).

In this section also he talks about the important nature of calling, or vocation. If we have been called from a life of sin, we may have great doubts that we can persevere. What has brought us to our knees may not be enough to keep us humbled for a lifetime. We have little energy from past, now-dead relationships to power a long-term change. Shame and guilt will not likely sustain us during a lifetime of effort. However, we may have experienced a much stronger call than that provided by shame or guilt. We may have heard an inner call to give everything. This was the call the monastics heard when they heard the call to celibacy (*Conf.* III.4).

They explained this call in several ways. The early monastic fathers taught that if Christ has entered a person's soul, and that person is one with Christ's Mystical Body, his soul enlivened by the Holy Spirit, his body should be chaste, pure, holy, and one with God. Another motivation for celibacy had to do with the end of time. The *parousia* (Second Coming) or the reign of God, the early fathers felt, was immanent and therefore human beings should live in the world like the angels, standing in awe, with a clear consciousness of heaven. This path calls one from deep inside to go to God alone, without a partner. God alone satisfies our deepest urges.

The reason for monastic celibacy that makes the most compelling sense today is that the mind needs to be focused, without the complexities created by having and being responsible for a spouse. The focused mind meets God not only in heaven, but also in this life. The mind is stabilized through the sublimated sexual energies.

The desert tradition also teaches us that to pray without ceasing one needs to totally dedicate oneself to prayer and to live a lifestyle that supports the dominant work of the contemplative life: to pray always. One therfore cannot take on the obligations of an intimate relationship with another person. If we are to learn the Scriptures, we can have no other husband or wife. If we desire to reach purity of heart (passionlessness), we must have only thoughts of God in our consciousness. To experience God directly and become fire (ecstasy), the body needs all of its heat for prayer. Sex will cool its energies.

Religious life and married life are more alike than different. The sisters in my community do not exist to fill my intimacy needs; rather, they help me practice my total dedication to God. To say this doesn't mean that I do not love them. It means that I love them with purity of heart. If there is a healthy purpose in living so closely together, it is to reduce the ego. Emotions ebb and surge and, if we become conscious of our thoughts and learn how to control our thoughts, we can dismantle our unhealthy egos and do the loving thing. This is the practice of the monastery. This is also the interrelational work of married couples. Whether living in a household or a monastery our egos must be diminished for the sake of the larger good. Yet to diminish the ego isn't the goal of the spiritual life. The goal is love.

No persons exist for our exclusive use. Relationships produce mutual benefits. However, they also produce something greater than themselves. The fruit of a well-ordered affect produces a bond of "we." Cassian felt that these relationships, this "we"-ness, should be regarded as companions on the journey, not simply as ends in themselves.

He wrote a section suggesting that it would be beneficial sometimes to require a monk to take a day's journey from the monastery in order to reduce stress and allow him to return after such a journey to better relationships within the community (*Conf.* XII.2). Cassian states that this is a permission to be absent—not an expelling, a punishment, or an isolation technique. This monk is not to be denied Eucharist, or coming to the table. The leaving is for the sake of returning. It provides time for the monk to work the passions down to a less compulsive intensity. Evagrius, the teacher of Cassian, gives the following advice: Withdrawal in love purifies the heart. Withdrawal with hate agitates it.[2]

---

2. *The Mind's Long Journey to the Holy Mountain: The Ad Monachos of Evagrius Ponticus*, trans. Jeremy Driscoll (Collegeville, Minn.: Liturgical Press, 1993), 31.

Perhaps, as far as relationships are concerned, distance is the best way to quiet the passions. When thoughts and desires are out of control, a vigorous day-long activity in another environment moves the physical energies back into balance. Married couples need to work things out with words, but perhaps a physical day apart might prevent words that will be regretted later. Some stories talk about staying with the sacraments and not withdrawing from the Communion table when undergoing the fires of sexual passions (*Inst.* VI.3).

Celibate persons experience a definite surge of energy, a more than ordinary movement of the heart toward anything that matters to the heart. Celibates describe this as an apostolic love, much greater than their individual capacity. All sexually awake persons feel sexual emotions. Persons are attracted to other persons and "fall in love," whether in the monastery or in a household. But it is not enough to be celibate. We are all called to be chaste.

Chastity is the prerogative of the inner chamber of the heart. A chaste mind helps me catch my "sex thought" at the first instance and helps me refrain from indulging in desiring another's body for my own sexual needs. Chastity helps me simply be before God, in total surrender. When I love God with my whole heart, soul and body, chastity governs how I love. Chastity has to do with my soul.

Continence, refraining from sexual activity, is the first stage in sexual asceticism. It's an early stage, sometimes weeks, months, and years of no sex. This stage may correspond to external circumstances such as a death of a spouse, separation from one's mate, extended illness, or the process of childbirth. Continence is no sex for one reason or another. We are continent because of circumstances, but not by desire.

Monastic celibacy or marriage is the choice that governs our other choices about intimacy. It is a middle ground between mere continence and chastity. It has to do with our observable behavior based on our choices in life. It is a way of life. This choice of monastic celibacy or marriage governs my leisure activity, my dwelling, sleeping arrangements, and my social boundaries. Though the choice of lifestyle is often made (or not made) during adolescence, that choice needs to be reaffirmed again and again. Two important rules govern those choices: I avoid an environment that evokes the desire for sex not appropriate for my life's choices, and I avoid relationships that are similarly threatening. If I am a nun, for instance, I put a stop to any relationships that could potentially lead to the physical practice of the married arrangement. If I am married, I check other sexual relationships as contrary to my marriage vows.

Chastity, on the other hand, governs my innermost thoughts: The thought of sex rises and is dashed against the rock of Christ. When I choose to be chaste I lay aside all inappropriate sexual thoughts. The interior discipline of chastity requires me to refrain from the thoughts of sex, controlling sexual thoughts and desires which come from external stimuli and, even more importantly, from my unconscious mind, by refusing to entertain the train of thoughts that rouse my sexual passions. I notice my thoughts, my stream of consciousness, and choose to let them go if they are incompatible with my promises.

Isn't this dangerously close to repression of sexuality as if it were bad? Like food, sex is good but must be well ordered for a blessed and balanced life.

Appropriate practices to control "sex thoughts," then, include keeping a distance from outside relationships and environments that stimulate sexual excitement, thoughts, desires, or passions that are not appropriate to my vocation. I need to take a vigorous walk away from temptation. I need to be vigilant over my thoughts. Observing my thoughts as soon as I become aware of them, detecting the subtle feelings of the sexual pleasure zone, is important. A thought unaccompanied by another thought goes away. The thought comes again and again, but if I do not entertain the idea, it will diminish.

The practice of guarding the heart helps to offset the impact of sexual urges. The heart is the sanctuary where God dwells. To share our heart is a deep and personal action. Sex feels deep, but that is an illusion. Our union with God is deeper and stronger than sex. All emotions only rise and can be sustained for about five minutes, then they decrease in intensity. A practice that moves them down without incident is to drink a glass of water, take a brisk walk or to chant inwardly the name of God. No matter what method one uses, the practice is to notice the first inkling of desire and move it out of consciousness by laying the thought aside or saying a short prayer.

Most sexual urges start with wholesome, but undiscerned, thoughts regarding the goodness, beauty, or truthfulness of someone who is exceptionally attractive. Then comes the commentary about how good it is to fall in love, as if the experience of loving another helps me grow. If the attraction is healthy, then discerned love follows. If the attraction is not for me, I must let go of the thought. To guard my heart is to make an internal tryst with myself. My secret attraction to another is laid bare and my heart is put "on guard." The earlier the thought is caught on the screen of consciousness, the quicker I regain control.

Self-deception abounds. The practice of disclosing one's innermost thoughts to another is a helpful practice to avoid such deception, but it must never be to the object of one's fantasy, the potential lover. Another wise elder is preferable. Raw emotions are tamed by humble admission. The early monastics practiced manifestation of thoughts (*exagoreusis*), laying their thoughts out to another (*Conf.* II.10). The practice was simple. The monastic would manifest his interior thoughts in an external forum, to his abbot. No analysis. No storytelling.

Just laying out the thought in a safe, sacred space: "Dash your thought against a rock." The abbot or an elder would listen with a discerning heart.

Abbot Moses warns not to trust an elder because of his age or gray hairs: Just as all young men are not alike in the fervor of their spirit nor equally instructed in learning and good morals, so to, we cannot trust that all old men are equally perfect and excellent. For the true riches of old men are not to be measured by gray hairs but by their diligence of their youth and the rewards of their past labors (*Conf.* II.13).

Cassian goes on to describe a good adviser. When an elder is recommended to us that person should be known by the fruits of his or her life. Has he or she struggled with afflictions and thoughts, and calmed the mind? Can he or she read hearts? Can he or she actually see into another's heart and not have a preoccupation with himself or herself?

Elders are in short supply in our day. What shall we do? Cassian tells of a similar question put to Abbot Mosses (*Conf.* II.10). His reply was that it is good for the disciple to lay out thoughts regardless of the elder's worthiness so that humility is practiced. But the monastic should not necessarily imitate the elder's life. Today we could perhaps say that, though we may not have the teachers, we do have the teaching.

But what if we get teachings that confuse us from the elders? For example: What is the foundational thinking surrounding masturbation? Does release of sexual tension lead to a healthier psychological life? This is a delicate matter and utmost discretion is necessary. In the spirit of the teachings on the second renunciation, self-sex is to be avoided. Arousal is natural and simply is. To self-stimulate contradicts the practice of noticing thoughts and laying them aside. Chastity requires this discipline. The normal and natural gift of grace will anticipate the movement from continence to celibacy and finally to chastity, to a living, conscious, awareness of God.

Many stories from antiquity have a twist of humor and a punch-line which points toward the underdog. There was a monk who went to his elder for advice on sexual passions. The elder got violently angry with the monk and said that no such thoughts can be tolerated. The monk was dejected and felt that he could no longer stay faithful to his vows. He fled the monastery. The elder also soon got afflicted with sexual arousal as a steady state. The elder went to Abbot Moses and asked what he should do? Abbot Moses told him to love the young monks and be empathetic. The elder at once saw his hypocrisy and his affliction subsided (*Conf.* II.13).

An abba or amma is always extolled for his or her compassionate understanding about how difficult it is to be pure in body, mind, and spirit. The desert fathers and mothers contended that there are no unforgivable sins and there is, therefore, solidarity with the struggle because until the last breath there are none who are spared this conflict. Sexual energy that is ripe for mating and procreation generates spiritual sons and daughters who feel the love of their spiritual fathers and mothers.

The above practice of laying out thoughts, called "manifestation of thoughts," is recommended by Abba Moses (*Conf.* II.10). True discretion is secured by humility. Thoughts laid out before the elder demonstrates willingness to be open, to change and to follow the will of God. The elder gives a "word" of salvation. The 2,000 sayings of the desert abbas and ammas are listed in the literature as *Apophthegmata Patrum* or *Sayings of the Desert Fathers.*[3] This word of the abba or amma was intended to go to the heart and unlock the cycle of thoughts that kept the

---

3. *Apophthegmata Patrum*, Anonymous Series, No. 221, trans. Benedicta Ward, *The Wisdom of the Desert Fathers* (Oxford: Fairacres, 1975) or *The Sayings of the Desert Fathers*, Alphabetical Series 13, trans. Benedicta Ward (Cistercian Publications, 1975), 3.

seeker stuck. The elder, who had already mastered thoughts could "read hearts" and knew the word(s) that would penetrate to the afflicted level of consciousness. So the seeker practiced manifestation of thoughts in all humility. The elder practiced discernment, mediating the word of God for the afflicted one.

Another practice to control sex thoughts was to say a short prayer inwardly instead of thinking about the thoughts. Cassian presents his favorite short prayer, "O God, come to my assistance. He teaches the practitioner to use this short prayer at all times of the day in all life's events when we need to turn to God (*Conf.* X.10). The tradition of "praying without ceasing" is very beneficial for one who strives for chastity in his quest for union with God. The purpose of the spiritual life is union with God. The most often recited prayer, the Jesus Prayer, said continuously, comes from this impulse, almost becoming as natural as breathing. Eastern Christian spirituality has kept this tradition alive. "Lord, Jesus Christ, Son of the Living God, have mercy on me, a sinner."

Learning from his teacher, Evagrius, Cassian advised close attention to dreams that conjure up images (*Conf.* XXII.3f). Dreams reveal unconscious activity, mostly repressive responses to life's situations. Noticing dreams anticipates conflicts which may rise in our consciousness. Sometimes dreams indicate still unresolved past conflictual relationships.

In regard to dreams, spiritual direction has four guidelines: The first is to pray just before sleep. The second is periodically to practice all-night vigils, i.e., experience the night and pray through the temptation in a periodic rhythm, thereby dispelling the challenges of night and darkness, keeping vigil over one's thoughts. In the *Philokalia*[4] a vigil is defined as

---

4. *Philokalia*, Vol IV, trans. G. E. H. Palmer, Philip Sherrard, and Kallistos Ware (London: Faber and Faber, 1995), 437.

the opposite of a state of drunken stupor, so that one experiences spiritual sobriety and alertness. To be vigilant signifies an attitude of attentiveness over inward thoughts and fantasies, maintaining guard over the heart and intellect.

The third directive is to fast and to still one's spirit, rising early and rededicating oneself to prayer. Fourth and finally, reduce any compulsive behavior such as too much food or drink that might catch you off guard.

The above are teachings articulated by John Cassian. Other teachings, however, can be extrapolated from his basic wisdom.

It's good for my spiritual life to get the sexual issue settled: Should I be a monk or nun vowed to celibacy, or a married partner and hence, celibate except for my designated beloved, or am I called to be a single or lay practitioner without a partner, but at home with myself without courting the next lover at every waking moment?

A matter for our times is for each person to square off with one's heterosexual or homosexual orientation. One can discern this by honestly facing the inner object of one's own fantasy, whether that is someone of the opposite sex or of the same sex. As with thought about food, my interior thoughts about sexual intimacy can dominate the whole of my consciousness. These thoughts freeze me in endless thinking. Not only can I not love God with my whole mind, body, and soul, but I cannot love anyone else either. My thoughts get turned back to myself over and over again. The loop goes nowhere and locks the ego to the self. If I am looking for a mate in each person who walks through the door, or if I am preoccupied with the thought of getting my sexual longings satisfied, spiritual awareness is dim. The interior life is about union with God and being in service to others. Sexual urges pull me back to self-reflexiveness. The ego is served, the self is dominant, and we are busy working for gain. Ultimately this kind of interior agenda is unsuitable for the spiritual life. The false self is shored up once again. Sex is good, but like food it can consume me rather than nourish my body, mind, and soul.

In short, the interior life can be consumed with seeking a mate rather than seeking God as God. Remember the three renunciations: first, I renounce my former way of life; second, I renounce my interior thoughts; and third, I renounce even the image of God in order to meet God as God is. The benefits of all three of these renunciations elude me if I am still negotiating my sexual agenda. Even gender consciousness must be transcended for the sake of a spiritual life with God, who is neither male nor female.

A few words about groups. On the spiritual journey groups mediate God. But if it's tricky to know one's self, it's even trickier to know a group. In the practice of manifestation of thoughts, the same advice holds for a group as for an individual. To lay one's thoughts out to a group is a practice of humility, though depending upon how enlightened the group is, one should be cautious about their "word of salvation." Group processes that are aimed at the first renunciation of leaving one's former way of life of alcoholism or drug addiction, have wonderful benefits to ready seekers for the spiritual journey. But just as physical, emotional, or mental abuse from individuals is to be avoided, however, so are these abuses to be avoided from groups. Cults are closed groups. Secrets provide a clue that there is something to hide. Another clue that the group is not going in the right direction is if a leader requires adulation or some kind of special bonds as a price of membership. Discernment is essential. Again, in the second renunciation the practice is overtly spiritual, training the mind for the sake of union with God.

Meditation is an essential practice in the control of sex thoughts. It is through meditation that we work on our unconscious motivations and compulsions, going deeper and deeper with steady practice. But we cannot meditate until fundamental way of life questions are answered. It matters for a practice if we sleep alone or with a mate (either physically or psychologically). If I am a beginner the external environment is important to help me know my thoughts. To practice manifestation of thoughts, prayer without ceasing, meditation, or *lectio*, my bedroom must be in order. Then my desires, though never silent, are at least ordered. My body is where I practice. Passions can be stilled there. Ever mindful that inner longings die with my last breath, I trust that, through practice, my body, mind, and soul even in this lifetime can be at peace.

Is this teaching too lofty? The chaos of our times points to the result of inattention to our thoughts about sex. All major religious traditions have teachings on thoughts. Thoughts matter for the spiritual journey. A lifetime practice of controlling thoughts, of seeking chastity, whether married or monastic, teaches us that respect and genuine love are possible, indeed inevitable for the spiritually alive. What I resist is the dominating power of my hungers, urges, and instincts.

But, what if I want to heighten my sexual desires because they give me energy and zest for life? Chastity provides a way to do that, an invitation to be one with oneself, with another and especially with God. At my innermost core I must move against my wounded self and my ego, and move toward my true self, the truth within me. I extend my hand to another and love others with honest mutuality. This kind of love makes our whole self turn to God who has first loved us. Note that the motive for chastity is not frigidity nor fear of sex, but total dedication of all my energies to love God with my whole body, mind, and soul. The fruit of this is selfless apostolic service.

To review, continence is no sex. Celibacy is a monastic promise and marriage is a promise of sexual union with one partner. Chastity is thinking pure thoughts. No one is the object of my intimacy needs. All thoughts are to be redirected to my heart's desire, which is to seek God. From this free and unencumbered energy flows true love and a great passion to do anything on behalf of the Beloved. Sexual energies are integrated in a higher state of consciousness and the body readily cooperates with renewed vigor, enthusiasm, and passionate devotion. If I were married, sexual love would be abundant. If I am single, then the energy is sublimated to wholehearted selfless service to others and devotion to God through community.

John Cassian has no explicit treatment of kundalini energy. In some traditions this energy is described as an attempt to move sexual energy toward religious consciousness. I believe the Christian preference is to sublimate sexual energies through a lifestyle of restraint. Celibacy that leads to chastity is the sexual practice that moves all the sexual energies toward mysticism. This movement is not unlike the Dalai Lama's prescription for contemporary Tibetan Buddhist monastics or the teachings of the Ramakrishna Society in Hinduism. The *Pantanjali Yoga Sutras* say:

> When one becomes steadfast in abstention from incontinence, he or she acquires spiritual energy. Sexual activity, and the thoughts and fantasies of sex, use up a great portion of our vital force. When that force is conserved through abstinence, it becomes sublimated as spiritual energy. Such energy is indispensable to a spiritual teacher; it is the power by which he transmits understanding to his or her pupils. For true religion is not "taught," like history or mathematics; it is transmitted, like light or heat."[5]

Some spiritual practices in Tantric yoga utilize the sexual energies in a systematic way. One of the reasons this practice may be dangerous today is that there are not many teachers

---

5. *Yoga Sutras*, trans. Swami Prabhavananda and Christopher Isherwood (Madras, India: Sri Ramakrishna Math, 1997), 104.

with enough spiritual powers to orchestrate those enormous energies. The effect on energy is the same, however, if one practices meditation on a steady, persistent, lifetime basis. Usually when kundalini energy is aroused, it is a clue that the person has not enough training for the practice. It is better to have that energy rise slowly, naturally, and be a part of one's apostolic love practice. When that happens, the energy points outward and not back to the self.

Cassian describes the disciple who has sublimated his or her sexual energy in *Institute IV.* The state that is produced by no sex, he says, has all the benefits of sex and more. In all these matters, the mind attains a subtle purity and will experience an increase of devotion that is difficult to describe or narrate. Just as one who has not experienced this joy cannot conceive of it, so too one cannot express it when one does conceive it. If you want to describe the sweetness of honey to someone who has never tasted it, that person will still not be able to experience with his ears what his mouth has never tasted. Likewise, those who have experienced the joy of the taste can only wonder at it within themselves. Thus, one with a quiet mind is inflamed with the words of the psalmist, "Wonderful are your works, and my soul is pleased to know them" (Ps 138:14). Cassian describes the heavenly infusion of spiritual joy by which the despondent spirit is quickened to inspired gladness; those fiery transports of the heart and the ineffable and unheard-of consolations of joy by which we are sometimes aroused from an inert and stupid torpor to most fervent prayer, as from a deep sleep (*Conf.* XII.12).

Chastity is heart work. One of the fruits of a chaste life is to be innocent. My soul is open and my heart is not divided. No secrets, no inner desires are kept from God or my spiritual director. No duplicity exists in me. I am naked to myself, to God (and to my spouse, if married) and what others see is what they can trust to be really so. The heart is at peace. The fruit of a chaste life is to seek God right now, right here because the self is wholly present. Awareness leads to insight and creative energy.

The thought "about sex" often is a lifetime issue. The next thought that must be considered seriously on the spiritual journey is the thought "about things." John Cassian has a long section on the proper use of things. His teachings are surprisingly gracious.

4. About Things

From a spiritual point of view, owning anything is an illusion. At best, all we do is use a thing. However, we desire, obtain, use, and secure more and more of them. This "getting of things" tends to fan the fire of desire to get more things the next time. Things are more seductive than sex. Things beget things. Thoughts "about things" seep into our consciousness image by image until we are overwhelmed with a desire for possessions. The proper spiritual attitude is to reverse this grasping inclination. Yet, we all need things, use things, and give and take things for our personal benefit.

This teaching about things is not about things in themselves. It points primarily to our personal attachment to things. Since it is an illusion to own anything, the proper relationship with things is to use them with permission of the Creator. I take care of things because these objects are gifts on loan to me, not because they are mine. The practice "about things" is a practice of detachment from them and wise use of them. The motivation behind the practice, which springs from a profound worship of God, Maker of heaven and earth and Creator of all living beings, including humankind, is to use things reverently rather than to own them. Creation is God's gift for all creatures to use.

The teachings of John Cassian are clear and instructive for all practitioners even though they were given to monastics about monastic life. The myth of Creation is played out in miniature in the monastery: The monk and the abbot play the roles of creature and Creator, respectively. The monk promises to renounce the "ways of the world" and return to God, reversing the myth of the Garden of Eden and reordering life entirely in order to seek God. The Genesis account of Creation and the Fall recounts the act of man's disobedience, of wanting to be like God. Man is initially at home with God and, after the Fall, becomes homeless, wanders the earth, seeking only to return home. The monastery symbolizes a second chance to live a right-ordered life, at home with God.

A sign of this coming home was the welcoming rite when the monk puts on new clothes, and is invested with the monastic habit. The exponential growth of a desire for things was keenly known by the monastics of the fourth century and they practiced total renunciation. A monk received everything from the monastery. No one person had anything of his own, yet he had everything for his use. He renounced his former way of life. His old clothes and all his former things he gave to the poor or to the monastery.

Monks considered private ownership the root of all evil, which, once begun, is very difficult to eradicate. Amassing things is a learned behavior, not a natural instinct. If grasping for things is learned, then it can be unlearned. I can avoid amassing things, but that is very difficult to do once I have begun to acquire them, and, more importantly, have acquired a taste for them. There are few good stopping places—one thing leads to another.

Monastics felt covetousness, the love of money, even a small amount of money, could make a soul lukewarm. The purpose behind their practice "about things" was to order the things in our life toward the desire to seek God. Cassian gives us a wonderful description of the monk infected with avarice, describing that affliction in this way:[1]

---

1. John Cassian, *Institute* VII, *On the Spirit of Covetousness* has thirty-one chapters. This list is a composite description I combined for the purposes of this book.

The truth of thought starts . . . "What is contained in the monastery it is not sufficient for me. The little that is given me can scarcely be endured . . . if I want a sound mind and sturdy body." *The train of thought goes on . . .* "What if my health deteriorates? They are careless about their sick. Clothes are insufficient. I'll need ways and means of travel if I need to see a doctor. Someone like me can't be supported like the poor without indignity." *And so he bamboozles himself with such thoughts as these . . .* "How can I get more money?"

Little desires grow:

"I want this for security".

"I want to double my money."

"I want to keep my assets safe."

"I want to have money so as not to toil by the labor of my hands."

"I want not to share so I keep my store of things secret."

"I'll need to work harder to get more and more."

"I will be mad if someone or something gets in the way of my plans."

"I'll need to move in such a way that things are secured quickly, easily, and to my satisfaction."

"I can keep this secret. No one needs to know. I can cover up the evidence so everyone will think I'm living the good monastic common life. In fact, some of my things I'll get from the common store and other things I'll have on my own supply."

"I will not reserve anything for the poor; I need all my assets to get set up. Later I'll give to the poor."

"I wish I had the things I had before I entered the monastery."

"I wish I had more contacts with rich people; I'll need to travel more to get better connected."

"I have wasted my best years in this monastery when I could have gotten rich and famous. Why was I so stupid?"

"Can I do special work (without knowledge of the abbot), to get money? How can I double my investment? Where shall I deposit it? With whom shall I entrust it? If it turns out well . . . my money can be put into a better investment. No amount of work is too much to take care of my things and money. When I retire I'll need this heap of money, and this isn't enough to be secure. I'll need to leave the monastery to get more money."

Results: The one caught up with avarice has lied, kept secrets from the abbot, broken his promise of total renunciation, given way to bursts of passions, and even entertained the thought of stealing. No scruples about humility can be observed. "I deserve this."

Through it all, gold and love of gain become to him as a god, as the belly does to others. So instead of worshipping God, he worships idols. Passing over the image of God in his soul, this monk worships the image of an earthly emperor, stamped on coins. He chooses to love and care for things and not for God. This downward direction overshadows humility, charity, and obedience. He becomes displeased with honest work and casts off all reverence. Like a bad-tempered horse, he dashes off headlong and unbridled. This avaricious one becomes discontented with daily food and the clothing given him and thinks that salvation is better attained in other places.

A monk who has money cannot stay in the monastery. The monastic with many things teeters on the edge of the monastic way of life, and may be on the verge of leaving. He answers impertinently to commands and acts like a visitor who sees things like an observer, rather than as a member of the community. Whatever he sees that needs improvement he despairs of and treats with contempt, even though he has a hidden supply of luxuries for his comfort. He becomes indignant when things are given out slowly. If someone gives something first to another who has nothing, the avaricious one is inflamed with burning rage. "I'm treated like a stranger." Nor is he content to turn his hand to any work, but finds fault with everything which needs to be done.

And the train of thoughts goes on unrelentingly . . . He looks for opportunities of being offended and angry lest he might seem to have gone forth from the discipline of the monastery for a trivial reason. He tries to corrupt as many as he can by clandestine conferences and sows seeds of discontent. He highlights all the downsides and defects of the monastery. He murmurs at the slightest tasks that are required, but is indefatigable when working for his own gain. He is driven and inflamed with the love of money. Like a wild beast he is separated from the herd. He gives in to compulsion, then labors day and night, keeps no services of prayer, no system of fasting, no rule of vigils, no intercessions. He only wants, he feels, to supply his daily wants.

Instead he fans the fire of covetousness, while believing that it will be extinguished by possessing more and more. Soon one can observe that he has taken on a life that will soon be so complex, that to get out of it will be quite difficult.

The description continues . . . He loses sight of the present and is given to day-dreaming about things he either had or never had, but still longs for. Heightened anger comes often, either when thinking about things he had in his former life, or things he could have had if he had not entered the monastery, or things he is going to secure. He thinks about those future things over and over again in his waking moments.

The things he wants so desperately don't even exist because they are images in his mind. The monk lives with a double heart—one heart in the visible world and the other in the invisible world of desires and fantasy. He lives with the practice of seeking permission to use things, but in fact he lives with the desire and image of things either from the past or in the future "as if he owned them."

This dualistic life often gives way to choosing the single life leaving the monastery in search of things to satisfy his acquisitive passion and leaving behind the spiritual life of renunciation for the sake of seeking God. His god is now things. Covetousness is the worship of idols. What a downfall this madness leads to: step by step it leads to an actual worship of idols and false gods (*Inst.* VII.7).

Because the monks believed that avarice is a learned vice, they provided strong preventive teachings concerning things. Visible possessions, they said, are not our own. The earliest descriptions of Christian communities, referred to in the Acts of the Apostles, claimed that things are to be used for the whole community and stressed especially the need to distribute goods to the poor. The sad story of Ananias and Sapphira gives warning. Ananias and Sapphira secretly sinned, pretending to give all of their wealth to the Apostles but covertly keeping half for themselves. They both died as they were lying about giving up their wealth and are often used as examples of not being able to bridle their need for more things than what might have been distributed to them by the Apostles (Acts 5:1–12).

The desert elders, however, state that things are a means to invisible riches. They advise us to strive to possess the fruits of a detached way of life, a life that is free because it enables us to live within our means, enjoying a rich interior contentment with self, God, and others. Things, they say, are tools to mediate holiness. Obedience and humility guide us in their proper use. If we do not grasp things, our interior life of contemplation grows and develops.

Cassian tells us that the Christian tradition teaches that we cannot put an end to our desire for things by having a large or small sum of money. We can only do that by virtue of renunciation and he urges us to root out the desire to acquire as well as the wish to retain. No number of things can satisfy the grasping, greedy impulse of avarice.

This instruction about things may seem to be idealistic— a nice idea, but impossible to do. What practitioners report from experience, however, is that instead of being impractical, it is eminently doable. John Cassian realizes the weight of our human nature. When we consent to a serious relationship with God, grace follows. Cassian notes that none of us has to do all the practices of the spiritual life. But many who answer their inner light begin, through inclination after inclination, to make choices from a discerning heart. Over time, this practice becomes a lifestyle.

Cassian reminds his monks that the remedy for their avarice is to learn to depend on the monastery. They should get clothes and things from the abbot. They should get permission for what they need. In obedience, they should use things and return them to the common store. Things mediate the holy in the service of seeking God, and they should be grateful for what they have been given, free of worry and unencumbered because there is no watching and taking care of possessions.

Cassian goes on to stress the value of work in keeping a proper perspective about things. Common life means to share the work of the monastery, to do one's part in humility. Work is a tool for obedience and humility. Work secures enough things to live and surrender to God.

Work, he says, is good in itself (*Inst.* X.14). As a spiritual practice it is not done "to get something done." Being mindful of God's presence is, in fact, the interior work of my soul. The exterior work of my body provides the form through which I attend to my desire to forge an urgent relationship with God, one that will last for all eternity, but starts in the here and now. Work, therefore, is prayer (*Inst.* XI.24).

As a requirement to enter the monastery, the monk must have no ongoing benefit from things. He is to give all to the poor. True to this teaching the monastic doesn't give gifts to others because he has nothing more to give that he has not already given to the poor. He gives service from the monastery, however, through hospitality, and in this service receives Christ in the poor, the guest, the elderly, and the sick. If anything is given to the poor it is given in the name of the monastery

Cassian instructs the monk that he must never take back what he has renounced and has thoroughly eradicated the desire to possess. There are many stories of monks not making progress in prayer. The reason for this lack of progress, he says, is because the monk at first made a total renunciation of things, but gradually took them back, little by little, through the worldly practice of ownership either in fact or in his mind. He grew careless. Vigilance over incessant desires is the practice which prevents backsliding, since covetousness starts with little things and then grows into larger and larger ways of "being possessed by possessions."

The monk is to receive gifts and use them only with permission. They are never to be asked for by an individual, but only in the name of the community and then only if they are solicited for the good of the group. In the Christian tradition, a mendicant is one, like the Franciscans, the Little Sisters of the Poor, or Mother Teresa of Calcutta, who begs on behalf of others. The community is a safeguard to an individual's tendency to amass wealth. However, even the larger community must do self-audits from time to time.

In summary, John Cassian's teachings "about things" are themes and variations on this train of thought: It is an illusion to possess things. Even the thought of things needs to be rooted out. No thing can be owned since ownership is really an illusion of the mind. No number of things can satisfy our desire. Our desire needs to be rooted out. A monk will regard all utensils and goods of the monastery as sacred vessels of the altar, aware that nothing is to be neglected. He should not be prone to greed, nor be wasteful and extravagant with the goods of the monastery, but should do everything with moderation and according to the abbot's orders. In this way things can become a means to practice humility and obedience (*RB* 31.10).

A monastic's thoughts about things—whether they are material objects or "things I must do"—need to be focused on the single idea that God alone satisfies. As long as one's thoughts are filled with "things" the mind is fragmented and its energy out of control. Desire can be lessened by redirecting the first inkling of desire for things which appears on the screen of consciousness to living totally in an awareness of God's presence.

Can an ordinary Christian practice these directives in the world? I believe these teachings have implications for postmodern seekers. They encourage me to stay involved with a Christian community that values sharing goods, reaching out to the poor, and caring for all the goods of the earth. They call me to refrain from thinking about "my things," to pray for discernment about the right use of things for the honor and glory of God. The heart is the mirror of the One we are seeking. If in my heart there are only material and self-made things, I will not see God there. Ultimately the more things I have, the more cloudy and unclear the mirror becomes.

Reflecting on the memory of God is a major theme in antiquity. When the seeker thinks of God she becomes aware of creation and is grateful: and prayer rises. This gratitude for the book of nature is similar to the activity of *lectio* or reading, during the fourfold process of *lectio divina* that we use to study and pray over the book of Scripture. We know that the memory of God is kept alive by continual gratitude because God is offering us new graces at every moment and because God's gifts, as seen through the book of nature, are beyond the limits of time, lasting forever.

God is imprinted in our hearts and we have access to him through our remembrance. It isn't as if he comes from somewhere "out there." God is closer to us than we are to ourselves. The faith-filled person makes a personal resolution, *politeia*, to follow a program, a "rule of life," that makes it a habit to remember God. This is the origin of the word of politics, that resolve that we make with our full consent. This resolution might take the form of a short prayer whenever we notice beauty in God's creation. Eventually we find ourselves in a state of gratitude walking "in the Presence of God." This is the positive practice (asceticism) which is linked with the more negative practice of controlling our thoughts about things. Instead of thinking about things, we remember God.

Can I then just think about God and forget the discipline? Evagrius, the teacher of Cassian, said that there is no other way to contemplation than a praxis (practice) about the thoughts. Cassian says, "If one wishes to go from vices to virtues and through virtues to union with God there is no other way" (*Conf.* XIV.2). The Greek term for the monk's "way of life" was *praktké* translated as "practice." The implication for those of us who live in the most affluent country in the world is that as we must practice by laying aside our thoughts about "things," we must shift our thinking, instead, to the memory of God, to remembering the Beloved's presence within us. With grateful hearts must we lift up prayers of thankfulness and mirror God instead of things. Our life becomes a worship, and ritual mindfulness replaces worry and anxiety.

A healthy marriage demands the same as a monastic practice of total renunciation. All is shared. The family pools assets. Priorities are established. Each person yields to the common good while personal needs are met as well as they can be. The household is the monastery. Goods are shared

2. Irenee Hausherr, *The Name of Jesus* (Kalamazoo, Mich.: Cistercian Publications, 1978), 158 ff.

according to need. Things mediate love and compassion. Things are not owned, but are tools for charity. Desire for things has no grip. Desires are redirected to responsible action on behalf of justice for others.

Things and desire for things often feed on our soul. When we are deprived of things, anger can arise within us. Is this a sign that we need things for healthy development? What happens when one doesn't have the things that one needs? As we continue, we will visit the teachings of antiquity "about anger."

5. About Anger

The thought of "about anger" rises in each one of us. Anger is a response that is frequent, habitual, and sometimes seems apparently uncontrollable. We often adjust to bouts of anger in ourselves and in others. John Cassian recognized that in order to live the spiritual life, we must reduce our angry impulses, refrain from acting out our anger, and strive to resist even the thought of anger. According to the desert fathers and mothers, anger is a learned behavior and can be unlearned. This Christian teaching says we act rightly and justly, never out of angry feelings. Cassian continues with explicit directives:

In the context of original sin, anger is a consequence of the cumulative sin we have inherited. If we heap our own anger upon others, the cycle continues. However, the grace given to each baptized Christian reverses this tendency. In the spiritual life, through grace, I am able to root out anger from my heart.

"The eye of the soul is deprived of the light of right judgment and discretion," say the ancients. Anger diminishes the insight which springs from an honest gaze. If I am full of anger I am blind; I have lost the capacity to give proper counsel and no longer enjoy the confidence of right thinking and acting. My spiritual capacity is diminished and true light is dimmed within me. I start quarrels and lose the esteem of others. The most compelling indictment against anger is that this blindness disqualifies me from spiritual work since I am out of relationship with myself, with others, and with God. I cannot discern. If that is not enough to give me pause, the teaching goes on to say that unchecked anger leads to depression, madness and universal disharmony. The corrective is to seek peace and to do the interior work necessary to dismantle angry thoughts.

The goal of the seeker is purity of heart. I was created by God and, if I am a seeker, my desire is to return to God who is love. Before I can "see God," however, my heart must be transparent and this transparency of heart is the fruit of *apatheia*, the stilling of the thoughts. Thoughts come and go, but if I linger on a thought, this thought places an obstacle between me and union with God.

Origen (186–255) is famous for his use the image of a journey to describe the spiritual life. Origen used the term the "active life" to refer to a practitioner's work of controlling his or her thoughts (the work of asceticism), and described the "contemplative life" as the life of pure prayer. Both the active life and the contemplative life, he felt, were experienced by every seeker. These distinctions shifted over time, however, and these notions were handed down in a very different way to our generation. The active life that attended to internal thoughts was lost and is now defined almost exclusively as exterior apostolic work, while the contemplative life is defined, as it was earlier, as consisting in the interior life of prayer.

If I understand Origen's theories correctly, there are two forms of the active life and two forms of the contemplative life:[1] Evagrius, the teacher of John Cassian, built upon Origen's distinctions of the active and contemplative life and made them two successive stages. By moving through the thoughts one would achieve "pure prayer." Evagrius was the one who defined prayer as "lifting up of the mind to God" and as "the expulsion of thoughts." This meant all thoughts and

---

1. *The Rule of Saint Benedict 1980*, ed. Timothy Fry (Collegeville, Minn.: Liturgical Press, 1981), 36–38.

images would be purged and then the mind could be filled with the light of the Holy Trinity; one lost self-consciousness and attained a state of spiritual ecstasy which Evagrius called <u>anaesthesia</u> (Evag. *de orat.*120).[2]

The active life:
1. The negative form of the active life is to control the influence of the eight classic thoughts upon me.
2. The positive form is to practice the virtues instead of vices.

The contemplative life:
1. The positive form of the contemplative life is to come to know God, wherein I affirm all the goodness, beauty, and love of God in creation and all that I know by reason. This is the way of knowing that informs the intellect that God is beyond all forms and images.
2. The negative form is the way of unknowing or ignorance. The human senses of the intellect are incapable of attaining God. The divine darkness is the unapproachable light in which God is said to dwell. All one can do is prepare through prayer and purification because union with God is not attained through human wisdom but is a divine gift. We must be empty to receive this both immanent and transcendent One.

Since oversimplification through the years has caused the active life to be interpreted only as external charitable works of apostolic outreach, the negative practice of the active life—the interior work of renunciation of thoughts—was deleted. One's search for God through prayer became the only contemplative work. As the desert tradition became more obscure, Christian contemplatives were taught to practice prayer, but were given no training about controlling their

---

2. Ibid., 44.

thoughts. Distractions at prayer were a primary concern, but there were no practical suggestions about how to deal with them. For those in the active life, the practical "thought wisdom" of the desert tradition was reduced to the seven capital sins that all Christians should avoid for fear of eternal damnation. In effect, active apostolic seekers were exhorted to be virtuous without any training of the mind, and contemplative seekers were taught to pray without any tools.

The struggle with thoughts is an ascetical practice that moves us through the purgative stage in order to remove things that blind us (a moral stage). Once thoughts are under control, the illuminative stage can emerge (assimilation of truth). We see the light! Our hearts are pure and our minds are clear. With further training we learn to refrain from overusing our reasoning faculty and we move into an abiding love of God that is beyond our human concepts of God (mystical union, strict sense of contemplation).

With this teaching in mind the monastic catechesis on anger is a critical passage on the journey. The teaching on anger poses a clear directive: The monastic should be calm. Anger does not befit the chosen vessel called to seek God. Anger opposes purity of heart, *apatheia* (stillness of thoughts), and peace. Pure prayer qualifies me, through discernment or discretion which give me a clear vision, to be of benefit to others.

Discrimination (*diakrisis*) is a spiritual gift that permits one to discriminate among the types of thoughts that enter one's mind, assess them accurately, and treat them accordingly. Through this gift, one gains "discernment of spirits," the ability to distinguish between those thoughts or visions inspired by God and those suggestions or fantasies coming from the devil. Discernment provides an eye or a lantern within the soul, by which we can find our way along the spiritual path without falling into extremes; thus it includes the idea of moderation (*Philokalia*, vol. IV, 429). Charity springs up and happens naturally, for instance, but is prevented by anger.

Therefore, anger must be entirely rooted out. We must not hold on to even a little anger because, "It makes no difference whether gold plates, or lead, or what metal you place over the eyelids, the value of the metal makes no difference to the blindness" (*Inst.* VIII.6). Blindness is blindness. One can't see. Anger may be caused by a minor incident or a major crime; that makes no difference to a practitioner. Any anger causes distraction and misguided actions. When I am angry, both my own soul and that of another person are equally inaccessible.

Being aware of our angry thoughts is healthy. Like all emotions, anger provides information to our consciousness. We know how we think and feel, and we have responses ready for selection and operation. When I have been hurt by someone, I can respond with compassion. The energy produced by inclinations toward anger can be redirected in order to select a more appropriate response to the situation. In wrestling with anger I can learn humility—Why should someone treat me with special deference?, I can ask myself. Anger can be an indication of attachment to the self and the incident that provoked the anger may give me the opportunity to practice patience.

As I read this teaching from the desert tradition, Cassian does not use the passage about Jesus in the temple overturning the tables in order to justify "legitimate anger," or the beginnings of a "just war" theory. The emphasis, he tells his monks, is on the pursuit of purity of heart and contemplation. I must work full time on stilling my thoughts. Another's bad action may call for a "work of justice" on my part—for instance, moving out the money-changers—but I must do that action from a "heart center," and not from an "anger center." Actions to effect justice should look, feel, and be nonviolent.

There are five themes in John Cassian aimed at offsetting, reducing, and ultimately ridding the practitioner of anger and providing a sturdy basis for discernment.

Vigilance: The sun should not set on wrath because, "as in a murky night" my anger will rise stronger than before. Cassian advises me not to permit anger, even for a moment, to enter my heart because when I repress anger I will find that for several days I will not speak pleasantly nor with civility. When anger arrives all my thoughts silently feed on it. Then two things happen: I have thoughts of revenge and getting even, and I do not pray. I am no longer the temple of the Holy Spirit. Anger excludes the radiance of the Holy Spirit.

Reconciliation: Though exceedingly difficult, a ritual of forgiveness is absolutely necessary. I must postpone my prayer, "for anyone's loss is a loss for all of us" (*Inst.* VIII.14). I cannot pray if I am aware that a brother or sister has anything against me. Notice that this teaching takes the scriptural command literally. It is not about reaching out to someone who has wronged me. It is about reaching out to someone who has something against me. I might be innocent. Even if I am falsely accused, I can respond for my own as well as my accuser's benefit, rather than react to another's insult. In practice, this is very difficult to do, since a premature peace may place salt on the wound, and make matters worse. St. Benedict warns us against making a false peace. Perhaps the most I can do is soften my heart in order to get ready to make peace so that when the right time comes I will have a heart prepared to reconcile. The point of the directive is to anticipate another's anger. I am willing to reconcile even before the other is, and this helps to not escalate the situation, becoming a sound basis for a harmonious community.

Memory: Cassian tells us that we should root out all anger, hatred, and thoughts of retaliation. More than this, we should root out all memory of such things. Once we have forgiven, he says, never go back. The practice is to forget as many times as it takes to move the thought of anger out of my consciousness. To forgive but not forget is against the spirit of reconciliation. The practice is to rid my interior thoughts of the memory of the incident, words, or series of events that provoked my anger. I am to rid my thoughts of any perceptions and commentary about the event. Each time I feel anger, I am to redirect any thoughts associated with the feeling, and return to thoughts of charity and compassion. Such actions are a profound reminder of my own weakness and need for God's grace.

Solitude: It might seem that I should distance myself from the person, place, or thing I am angry about, so I can cool off. The practice, however, is to face my anger, and stay in the relationships of my chosen lifestyle. The teaching advises against imagining that if I didn't live or work with so and so, then I would not be angry. I can't really blame others for impatience on my part. If I fancy solitude, where no one can provoke me, then I will soon discover that I am angry at things . . . a pen, a knife, a rock, or an obstacle on my path. Today I might feel anger at my computer, or at traffic. Anger is within my own self and needs to be rooted out.

Freedom: In our day it seems that anger is inevitable. Do I really have any ability not to be angry? In *Conference* I, Abbot Moses gives a revealing teaching about our innermost thoughts, desires, and passions. It is impossible, he says, for the mind not to be approached by thoughts, but it is in the power of every earnest man or woman either to admit them or to reject them. Their rising up does not depend entirely on myself, but the rejection or admission of them, does lie in my own power. He goes on to say that this acceptance or rejection of thoughts is the subject of free will and my efforts to control my thoughts lie in my own power. Either holy and spiritual thoughts, or earthly thoughts, can be allowed to grow in my heart (*Conf.* I.17).

He recommends frequent reading and continual meditation on the Scriptures, frequent singing of the Psalms, earnest
vigils, fasting, and prayer. These spiritual practices keep the
mind thinking noble thoughts and anger, lust, or greed have
little room to grow. Preferring spiritual realities (thoughts
toward God) over worldly concerns (thoughts toward the ego)
is what is often called recollection. Abbot Moses uses the
image of a grist millwheel which never stops but powers the
millstone to grind the grains into flour. Though the mind is
always turning, I can choose what kinds of grains I give the
mind to "chew" on. The goal is to remember God, to meditate. I am advised to pray and control my thoughts to such an
extent that God can communicate directly to my soul—without thought. That is contemplation.

Recollection: To reach this level of contemplation, recollection must prevail. A wonderful section in *Conference* IX
says about thoughts: whatever I think about before prayer
comes into church with me. All my images, concepts, and
stored feelings walk to the pew with me. On the outside I
may look like I am praying, but on the inside I am engaged
in previous conversations. Even though the setting is different, my feelings rise exactly in the same way: anger, sadness,
sexual desires, and greed come at me with the same, or even
stronger force, when I enter church. Not every thought or
feeling is on the downside. I may be celebrating a promotion
or a friendship, or remembering a good joke. It is all the
same. I am not present to myself. I can't lift my heart and
mind to God. Prayer really isn't possible. Therefore, the
directive is to "get recollected" or ready to listen; to open
myself to hear from the inside and the outside the word of
God in Scripture, in sacred music, or even in that provoca-
tive language of silence. To pray without ceasing is always
very difficult, but to pray at all, anywhere, first of all takes
recollection (*Conf.* X.10).

Cassian reinforces, as essential to a life of prayer, the teaching of the middle renunciation. To contemplate, I must think of God. To think of Him, I must control my thoughts, a control that requires that I still my mind. This control is achieved by not-thinking, a practice whereby, each time I notice a thought, I return to silence. I may also accomplish it by returning to a sacred word or a sacred image or to my breath, using that word or image or breath like a feather that releases the thought, letting it go with each breath and each heart beat. My effort is to direct my heart toward a sacred intention. Prayer requires my intention to love God—a quiet, wordless intention. As articulated a thousand years later in that classic, *The Cloud of the Unknowing*,[3] prayer happens in this silence because God is beyond thoughts and images. Purity of heart is simply a clear mind without thoughts In this clear mind, charity springs up without effort.

In *Conferences* IX and X, Abbot Isaac gives the most thorough description of pure prayer found in the Christian tradition. The practices concerning thoughts about food, sex, things, and anger, he says, are ascetical prerequisites to enter into a deep spiritual life of union with God not sometime in eternity, but now, on this earth, during this lifetime. Conversely, a deep contemplative life devoted to prayer is not going to become a reality unless I do the interior work of controlling my thoughts. The practice of recollection requires me to continually turn my mind to God in prayer, seeking God in every corner of my thoughts. This search leads me to ask whether, when thoughts rise, these thoughts are from God, from my self, or from the devil. If I am angry I cannot discern. I can only feel anger, triggered by my angry thoughts. Stability

---

3. *The Cloud of Unknowing*, trans. Wm. Johnston (New York: Doubleday Image Books, 1973), 27.

of thought is most difficult even after anger subsides. To refrain from the lightness of one thought here and one thought there, one must train for constant attention (*Conf.* XI.12).

While this problem of discerning applies to all thoughts, anger is the most devastating of the thoughts because it leads so quickly and absolutely to blindness. I lose my power to judge rightly. Since thoughts rise unsolicited, my challenge is to redirect, edit, and cancel certain trains of thought. Which thoughts are helpful and lend beauty, grace, and zest for life? Which ones are deadly? John Cassian's report of the desert abbas and ammas devotes more than eighty pages to aspects of discernment. He stresses that we must attend to the source of our thoughts: Do they come from the self, from God, or from outside influences? Of what value is the thought? Some thoughts are good, others are bad, and still others are indifferent. What are the consequences? Where does the thought lead me? How do I know?

"Believe not every spirit, but prove the spirits whether they are of God" (Jn 4:1). Test and see if this thought is true or false. Is it good of itself, is it good for me, and is it good for me now? How can I verify that it is good?

Be adept at wise puzzlement because partial truths can be deceptive. Things are not always what they seem. A good that leads to vice may sometimes seem useful at first, but in the long run, it will weaken my resolve. An argument that the end justifies the means may be compelling, but wrong patterns may ultimately emerge. Thoughts may contain the right motivation, but the wrong emphasis. Shouldn't I be a little angry at injustices done to the poor? Shouldn't I be angry, like Christ was in the temple, with the money-changers? The teaching advises me to check to see if I am only half right. Am I discounting tradition, am I shifting the meaning slightly, weighing things differently? If so, my thoughts, my decisions, may not be true gold, tested and weighted so I know what I am getting in exchange. I may have the right idea but the wrong action.

Another aspect of discernment is to ask myself if my behavior appears as a sincere action but comes from the wrong motivation. An example would be that, though I do not retaliate for a perceived injustice, I nonetheless hold a superior attitude in my heart. Cassian tells us:

> We should constantly search all the inner chambers of our hearts lest, unhappily, some beast related to the understanding, either lion or dragon, passing through, has furtively left dangerous marks of his track. And so, daily and hourly, turn up the ground of our hearts with the gospel plough, i.e., the constant recollection of the Lord's cross. By doing so, we shall manage to stamp out from our hearts the lairs of noxious beasts and the lurking places of poisonous serpents. (*Conf.* II Abbot Moses, 22)

Discernment is not to be used only for major decisions, but is to be used also in ordinary circumstances. Though in more recent history, the tradition of discernment has become relegated to making only fundamental life choices, such as choosing a vocation to marriage or to religious life, discernment primarily encouraged the practitioner to develop a discerning heart, to use moderation in all things. Cassian taught that extremes meet. Having either too much or too little usually results in the same consequences in the spiritual life. All self-willed compulsions are to be avoided; gluttony or excessive fasting, for instance, are equally dangerous. Frigidity and hostility toward others are as bad as sexual fantasies that lead to lewd conduct. The middle road helps to keep me humble.

Great peace comes to me when struggle subsides. This absence of struggle is called equanimity, the harmonizing of all extremes. According to Maha Ghosananda,[4] equanimity

---

4. Maha Ghosananda, *Step by Step* (Berkeley, Calif.: Parallax, 1992), 37.

creates a finely tuned instrument, not too tight and not too loose, vibrating perfectly and making beautiful music. Equanimity shows me that I am neither the greatest nor the least. In Cassian's time the abbot helped determine the middle path for the practitioner by taking into consideration the special needs and stages of each person.

Helpful to discernment is the practice of manifestation of thoughts (*exagoreusis*). By laying out my thoughts before an elder, I face my hidden thoughts and motivations, and I give the abbot or the elder a sense of where I am so that a middle course can be plotted.

How does discernment apply to thoughts about anger? If I am angry, I cannot discern because thoughts come too fast and are quickly distorted. I can't separate and make distinctions. Confusion follows. If I am angry, my heart shifts from a discerning heart to a fuming heart. I think only of my hurts and how I can get even with the perpetrator. I think only of justifying myself; my ego takes over. I lose sight of the real One, namely God, and patterns of prayer are blotted out in my rage.

If I let anger linger and feed it, I lose the capacity to interpret my actions rightly. I am unable to accept greater wisdom and I rely only on my own ego. I either become rigid or I disregard all boundaries. The middle course no longer guides my decisions. I lose the capacity to sort, to think, to pray, and to hold a dialogue with another for the purpose of gaining insight. If I am angry, I cannot be of use to others who need help in their decisions about relationships and courses of action because I am blind to myself, to others, and to God. Anger is costly. It needs to be rooted out at its first appearance on the screen of my consciousness.

But what if I'm right? If injustices should be stopped, shouldn't anger lead me out of passivity? Notice how active the process of discernment is. All of my thoughts are first observed, then edited, then redirected or canceled. There is no repression. There is no indifference. In my practice of discernment, if a thought arises about action on behalf of a victim, and this thought comes out of a center of truth and not anger, it is powerful and nonviolent. I act decisively, and wholeheartedly, with full compassion and charity. The work of an apostolic life is to relieve the lot of the poor. I work on behalf of justice. But I do this not out of the motivation of anger and judgment but out of the center of a discerning heart ready and willing to do whatever is necessary.

Judith Cebula, staff writer for the *Indianapolis Star,* quotes Mohandas Gandhi's grandson, Arun Gandhi (age sixty-seven, now living in Memphis, Tennessee) as saying he learned "from his grandfather how to recognize anger. That is the beginning of nonviolence—realizing you are angry and knowing the reason why." Gandhi said, "Grandfather taught me to write an anger journal, to write down my feelings whenever I was angry. Instead of putting the anger toward another person or thing, I poured it out into the journal to find a solution." Gandhi learned the connection between the passive anger of fear, prejudice, and intolerance and the active anger of fighting, killing, and warfare. British intolerance among India's Hindus and Muslims led to civil war there. In the United States, prejudice among blacks and whites and the growing divide between the rich and poor are polarizing American culture, Gandhi said. "All of these little fears become the foundation of violence, he said. All of us are responsible [for our anger]."[5]

Isn't anger natural in relationships? Doesn't anger show that I care? The following is a lengthy section on friendship from Cassian. Notice that he applies the teachings on the eight thoughts directly to friends. Therefore, we cannot

---

5. Judith Cebula, "Ghandi's grandson's stories teach Butler students about nonviolence," *The Indianapolis Star*, November 19, 1997.

avoid seeing that these teachings are meant to be applied directly to our own day-to-day relationships and are not merely lofty goals. Friendship, according to Cassian in *Conference* XVI, thrives on virtue, on harmony. Renunciation of thoughts provides a common ground. "There will be one purpose and one mind to will and to refuse the same things." To keep a friendship unbroken, he says, we must be careful that having first gotten rid of our faults and mortified our own desires, we can then be united with zeal and purpose so that we can diligently fulfill the delights of friendship. The union of friendship is, in fact, the union of characters. It is beneficial to be friends with one who loves fasting and feasting, who is chaste, and who uses things in common with no greed. It is good to be friends with one who resists anger and practices all the other ways of controlling thoughts that destabilize my mind.

The gift of friendship, says Abbot Joseph, can only last among those who are of equal goodness. They must share likemindedness and common purpose. They never, or hardly ever, disagree, or if they do differ, it is in matters which concern their progress in the spiritual life. But if they begin to get hot with eager disputes, it is clear that they have not made the three renunciations. For if they have truly renounced their thoughts then they could listen to another's thoughts without scorn (*Conf.* XVI.1–28).

The teaching goes on to state that the practitioner should never be angry for any reason, and that vexation toward another is equally bad for the practitioner. He should realize daily that he is to pass away from this world, and this realization will remove vexation and check sins of all kinds. When we live this way we don't suffer, nor do we cause suffering for others. But Cassian warns us that when the perspective about the fleetingness of earthly life fails, poison enters the hearts of friends. Frequent quarrels cool love;

friends first part their hearts, then their shared time and place. This is no surprise, since anger has begotten a long road of adversarial thoughts, desires, and passions.

Cassian goes on to note that if one has practiced renunciation of thoughts he will not argue with his friend: he claims nothing for himself, he cuts off the first cause of a quarrel, which generally springs from trivial things and most unimportant matters. If a friend practices holding all things in common (as did those in the Acts of the Apostles), then how can any seeds of dissension arise? A friend serves not his own desires but his brother's needs. Throughout this relationship he becomes like his Lord and Master, who says, "I come to do the will of Him that sent Me. By this shall all know that you are my disciples, as that you love one another" (Jn 15:17).

The conference of Abbot Joseph goes on: But on what grounds will the monk admit to the rancor between himself and his friend? None. There is no righteous anger because anger is dangerous and wrong. For when his brother is angry with him he cannot pray. And when he himself is angry with his brother he must practice forgiveness. "If you bring a gift to the altar and remember that your brother has anything against you, you must lay down your gifts and go to that brother and ask for forgiveness" (Mt 5:23–24). This is a serious charge for someone who has vowed to pray always. Cassian says, "It remains then either that we never pray at all, retaining this poison in our hearts, and become guilty in regard of this apostolic or evangelic charge, in which we are bidden to pray everywhere and without ceasing; or else, if, deceiving ourselves, we venture to pour forth our prayers, contrary to His comand, we must know that we are offering to God no prayer, but an obstinant temper with a rebellious spirit" (*Inst.* VIII.13). "Let not the sun go down upon your wrath" (Eph 4:26).

If I have an angry heart, these words cut me deeply, for in the same way I will be punished for violating the Lord's command. I must remember the briefness and fragility of life. How can I retain even the least vexation with my brother, when I realize daily that he is presently to depart from this world?

Anger is the most divisive emotion between friends: Put nothing before love. Abolish rage and anger. Disregard all things, however useful and necessary they seem, as secondary to friendship. Avoid anger. Undertake and endure all things so that the calm of love and peace may be preserved unimpaired. Nothing is more damaging than anger and vexation, and nothing more helpful than love. Even contention about spiritual things needs to be avoided. Remember, not only does love belong to God, but God is love!

There are different grades of love: family, associates, strangers, friends, and enemies create different opportunities to particularize love. In each instance the practice of forgiveness anticipates needs and extends love. Love is required of a believer who ultimately believes that the "other" is Christ. To act contrary to what prevents progress on the spiritual journey. Inappropriate behaviors such as passive–aggressive silence that provokes the other, or faking a peace that doesn't come from the heart, hurts both. Doing spiritual practices such as fasting, but a fasting motived by rage, is not only counter to seeking God, but can damage others as well as oneself (*Conf.* XVI.14).

Anger must be caught at its first instance because the nature of anger is such that when anger is snuffed out, it perishes. As in our attraction to possess things, "Watch for the tip of the serpent's head and be more keenly on our guard. For it it has been admitted (to our consciousness) it will grow by feeding on itself, and will kindle for itself a worse fire" (*Inst.* VII.21). But if anger is openly exhibited, it burns more and more brightly. The experience of days, months, and years without anger brightens the eyes, clears the skin, and quickens the walk of the seeker.

In summary, the goal is never to be angry at all, whether for good reasons or bad ones. If I am angry, I lose the light of discernment, the security of good counsel, and even the uprightness and temperate character of righteousness. I am a temple of the Holy Spirit. I ought never to pour out my prayer to God while I am angry. It is not proper to pray to God with anger burning in my heart. I can't love and hate during worship. If I nourish anger, neither renunciations, fasting, nor vigils will help me at all. To be moderate in food and drink, to use things wisely, to be celibate and chaste is difficult, but it can be done. However, anger can afflict the soul with such force that it negates all the earlier progress in the spiritual life.

The practice of discernment is to let go of my memories of wrong-doing. Recollection is a continual remembrance of one's goal on the spiritual journey and a mindfulness that reconciliation is possible, even if the other party is not aware of my loving thoughts. Reconciliation is a gesture of forgiveness. Grace anticipates the opportunity and provides the moment that makes reconciliation genuine, heartfelt, and lasting.

Cassian teaches that I have the tools to stay in relationships, and these tools help me remove thoughts of anger. This training of the mind is accompanied by peace and joyfulness. Love flows naturally, spontaneously and with a pure heart. The absence of anger enlightens the mind. I can more easily read the book of nature, the book of Scripture, and the book of experience. I learn that God is closer to me than I am to myself. My friends are manifestations of God. An eneffable joy replaces gloom, anxiety, and calculating about details that are out of my control.

I have free will, and even though I can't stop thoughts from rising in my consciousness, I can decide which thoughts I will entertain. Evagrius says that Whether all of these thoughts trouble the soul or do not trouble it does not depend on us. But whether they linger or do not linger or whether the passions move or are not moved, that depends on us" (*Praktikos* 6). Cassian teaches from the lips of Abbot Moses,

> that it is impossible for the mind to be approached by thoughts, but it is in the power of every earnest man or woman either to admit them or to reject them. As then their rising up does not entirely depend on ourselves, so the rejection or admission of them lies in our own power . . . to a great extent in our power (is) to improve the character of our thoughts and to let either holy and spiritual thoughts or earthly ones grow up in our hearts. (*Conf.* I.17)

He recommends *lectio*, singing the Psalms, fasts, and vigils to keep the mind stable. Friendship is sharing these spiritual practices. The bond of friends is precisely this desire to seek and meet God face to face as real as the face of the friend.

But what about anger, what do I do with it? When I notice violence I am willing and able to do whatever it takes to right it on behalf of justice. Though at times I don't know which way to turn, with prayer and discernment my path becomes clear and I am able to act decisively. When I act with a discerning heart I move with gentleness, charity, and compassion. As His Holiness, the Dalai Lama says, "My enemy helps me in my conduct of awakening."[6]

Recently, I gave a lecture about anger at the novice institute at Beech Grove, where Venerable Pema Tsultrim, a Tibetan Buddhist nun, was visiting. She reminded me that the Buddhists have a concept of *Bodhicitta* wherein the compassionate witch utilizes the practice of *Tonglen*: Give all profit and gain to others, take all loss and defeat on yourself. If the suffering is unjustified then there is all the more merit.[7]

---

6. Dalai Lama, *Healing Anger* (Ithaca, N.Y.: Snow Lion Publications, 1997), 97.

7. Sogyal Rinpoche, *The Tibetan Book of Living and Dying* (San Francisco: Harper, 1994), 193–205.

I realized that in my teaching that day I had missed the central sacrificial and redemptive core teaching of Christianity. Jesus died for us, raised us up, and bore our sins so that we are all blessed. This Buddhist teaching helped me see more clearly that, in accord with our main Christian teaching, we must anticipate one another's burdens and assume the role of sacrifice for the sake of another. To imitate Christ we must lay down our lives. The prerequisite to being able to do this is that I must get beyond anger in order to be able to pay the cost of discipleship.

This will become clearer when we study the teaching of humility surrounding the "vainglory thought." I am grateful to my Buddhist friend, Venerable Pema Tsultrim, for reminding me that this Buddhist tenet is exactly the same as the directive in our Christian way of life.[8]

Before we learn John Cassian's teachings about vainglory, however, we need to learn about dejection and acedia. Anger has another downside if it isn't mastered early in one's interior life. Anger can be turned inward and cause dejection, an affliction that is experienced as depression.

---

8. Pema Chödrön, *Start Where You Are: A Guide to Compassionate Living* (Boston: Shambala Publications, 1994), 50. This book describes Pema Tsultrim's point of view.

6. About Dejection

Cassian taught that dejection is built on anger. Sad thoughts lead to depression, to a state of being dejected. He went on to describe the qualities of dejection. Sometimes, he says, these woeful thoughts begin as attacks of random sadness, coming casually and haphazardly. Depression gains possession of my mind. This black mood keeps me from all insight. These sad thoughts utterly ruin and depress me. The murky night that settles inside my soul does not lift at sunrise. Melancholy becomes a steady mental state. Sleep brings no relief. I have fallen away from a state of purity (*Inst.* VIII.10).

Depression, Cassian continues, does not allow me to say my prayers with my usual gladness of heart, nor can I rely on the comfort I used to get from reading the sacred writings. I am impatient, and I can't be quiet and gentle with my brothers and sisters. In fact, I am rough in all of my duties of work and devotion. All wholesome counsel is lost and steadfastness of heart is destroyed. I feel almost mad and drunk. My mind crashes. I have overwhelming feelings accompanied with a deadly despair. Suicide becomes an option (*Inst.* IX.2).

Dejection is a condition provoked by thoughts, just as thoughts control our inclinations toward food, sex, things, and anger. It is very harmful to the human spirit. For "as the moth injures the garment and the worm the wood, so dejection is in the heart of man." The favorite image used to describe dejection is the image of being literally eaten away.

"It's gnawing dejection that eats away the priestly temple of the soul. Holes bore into my vestment or garment" (Prv 25:20, cited in *Inst.* IX.3).

How does dejection arise? The desert tradition offers three sources for "dejection thoughts" that lead to depression: First, depression is the result of previous *anger*. Second, dejection springs from a desire for gain that has not been realized: when we find that we have failed in our hope of securing those *things* we had planned for, we feel let down (*Inst.* IX.4).

The third point of origin is more mysterious. Dejection seems to afflict the victim without any apparent reason. Cassian notes that we can become suddenly depressed with so great a gloom that we cannot receive with ordinary civility the visits of those who are near and dear to us. We regard any subject of conversation started by our loved ones as ill timed and out of place. We can give them no civil answer because the gall of bitterness is in possession of every corner of our heart. But, he says, the kind of depression that seems to come out of nowhere deserves our utmost compassion for the victim. This kind of depression rises from underneath, with no cause to explain it. Today we would call this condition chemical depression, possibly a genetic disorder. The experience is hell, and the victim is innocent (*Inst.* IX.4).

Cassian notes that the origin of many cases of depression, however, is clearly in ourselves. We have stored up injured thoughts and feelings. Seeds from those thoughts start emotional memories growing with little provocation— memories that soon overpower our soul and burst forth into shoots of bad fruit, crowd our soul, and lead to an overwhelming sadness.

Cassian follows the pattern of thoughts attached to this deadly disease. Sadly we lament that our whole life of restraint has been a mistake. Perhaps we should have lived our life "as we pleased," at any cost to others. We begin to regret our life of resisting temptation. Thoughts that seem to have been hidden and concealed in our innermost soul now surface, causing heavy doses of regret and acrid cynicism. "Why didn't I leave and marry?" or "Why didn't I take that position of power and authority?"

What can we do? How is this depressed state of body, mind, and soul healed? Antiquity suggests five practices: *We should stay in relationship with others*. If I begin to isolate myself, there is no end to the number of people I cross off my list. People are bound to offend me often. Each person I know will offend me at some time or another, so if I isolate myself, the opportunity to practice patience, by bearing another's burdens, is lost. I may feel that some persons are better than I am, and it is painful to be with them. Or I may feel that I wish to change others who offend me. If I try to change people, at best I will just change the causes that separate me from former friends. But it is unlikely I will change them, and I will not change myself. As before, when the cause for depression seems to be from without, it is usually from within.

Cassian's advice regarding depression is the opposite of that given to one afflicted with thoughts of lust, who is told to flee: a different energy requires separation for the sake of reining in sexual frustrations. Again, an elder who has the gift of discernment can help with this decision. To isolate when one is depressed can lead to more confusion (*Inst.* IX.7).

Cassian goes on to advise those afflicted with depression: *We should do our best to amend our faults and correct our manners*. If I correct myself I will be at peace with people and even with animals (Job 3:23). I need not fear evil from without if I become aware of and admit the roots of my own evil. "For they have great peace who love your law, O God; and they have no occasion of falling" (Ps 143).

Refrain from thoughts that lead to self-destruction. Take these thoughts seriously. This affliction can lead to death, to self-destruction. To be alarmed at chronic, deep, dark thoughts is an appropriate reaction. Notice them! "Dejection thoughts" cause depression which can lead to suicide. An example from the Gospels is the Apostle Judas, who betrayed Jesus. He hung himself. There was an alternative: asking for forgiveness.

Refrain from and redirect any and all thoughts of putting oneself down. It is a form of pride to engage in thoughts that are emotionally laden with dejection. I really expected more praise, good fortune, better results than the reality of whatever happened. But what happened is the way it is, no more, no less. Thoughts that move beneath reality and back to the self with layers of commentary are against the spiritual practice of surrender, discernment, patience, humility, and obedience.

Resist morbid suffering. To suffer, imitating Christ who laid down his life for another, leaves no regrets, and calls one to do what is possible to change the situation for the better. To suffer as the world knows suffering, however, brings death (2 Cor 7:10). Morbid suffering faces toward the self. Contrary to living normally and getting on with daily activities and relationships, morbid suffering takes full advantage of the weight of sadness. This deadly experience gathers intensity, reaches below the conscious level of questions that afflict everyone at a certain stage of life. Morbid suffering has made a decision "not-to-care." In the tradition, however, suffering for the sake of suffering is not extolled. Patience wins the crown. Suffering is actually neutralized with acceptance and the grace of courage results.

Is dejection ever useful? Cassian taught that in some cases dejection can lead to compunction of heart and we can be inflamed with desire for perfection and contemplation of future blessedness. A fuller description of compunction is treated under the teaching about acedia in the next chapter. However, Cassian described this good form of dejection as that which works toward salvation. It is obedient, civil, humble, kindly, gentle, patient, and springs from the love of God Good dejection brings to my consciousness a persistent desire for perfection. Even bodily grief, and sorrow of spirit, can return my wandering heart to God. I rejoice and hope that suffering will profit me and preserve all gentleness and forbearance (*Inst.* IX.10).

How does the teaching help me detect and control the thought of dejection? How can I get ahead of that train of thought before it evolves into depression? Cassian notes that it is joyful to experience positive things in life. The classic list of positive things is contained in the fruits of the Holy Spirit: love, joy, peace, forbearance, goodness, benignity, faith, mildness, and modesty. Yet, sometimes I am not as quick to catch the insidious entry into my heart of those thoughts that lead to dejection. I do not detect these thoughts, but the fruits are read by others. As Cassian describes it: The dejected one shows signs of being rough, through displays of rancor and impatience. Each day the dejected monk grows more hardhearted toward others who need care and compassion. He displays useless grief and is caught in suicidal despair. This unwholesome sorrow draws out the energy from him and breaks down the one on whom it has fastened.

Because depression is unreasonable, if I am is caught in depression I am gripped by the tight fist of sadness. This sadness not only hampers the efficiency of my prayers, but in fact destroys all the fruits of the Spirit. An exchange occurs: instead of the fruits of the Holy Spirit, I experience the fruits of dejection.

About sorrow: Though sorrow ought to be checked to see if it belongs to the world that works toward death, some sorrow leads to life. The kind of sorrow we call compunction of spirit can move me to sincere grief for my wrong-doings or hardness of heart. Cassian describes thoughts of sorrow which sober the heart. I move closer to God by taking responsibility for the thought of sorrow and directing it toward the self that is seeking conversion. Compunction is wholesome sorrow. Dejection is unwholesome sorrow. When dejected, I get stuck, and stay in my sorry self rather than moving toward God. On the other hand, wholesome sorrow is aimed at the future and moves out of the self. It has a goal other than the self and is openly, wholeheartedly willing to make sacrifices in order to start again. I become mindful that life passes away, which makes me more mindful of how the details of life simply flow around life's vicissitudes. This realization helps me to detach from the painful experience.

How can I tell the difference between wholesome sorrow and compunction in my daily life? When I cycle around and around, thinking over and over about the harm done to myself, this is not healthy and I simply sink deeper and deeper into sorrow.

When I am deep in sorrow, is there a remedy? Cassian advises us to catch it early. Notice your thoughts. When you notice a sad thought say, "It just is: I feel sad. I count on God's grace." Then redirect the thought out of the consciousness. I may need to do this time and time again. Catch the thought early. Dispatch it. Dash it on the rock which is Christ. Since this kind of sorrow rises from the unconscious, utmost compassion needs to be my first concern.

How can we root out dejection? Isn't it a natural reaction to the bad things life brings us? Again, John Cassian advises us to resist all negative thoughts. Because of such thinking, depression can easily get the better of us. Things, he says, are neither up nor down. Life happens, and the mind, simply by observing reality, can move into equanimity. I have the freedom and grace to be able to expel negative passion from my heart. If, in meditation, I strive to keep my mind constantly occupied with hope for the future and with the contemplation of promised blessedness, I will also become hopeful now, in this life, because the Holy Spirit dwells within me.

Cassian insists that that we will all experience the thought of dejection that comes from resentment, disappointment, or loss, or even from an unknown disturbance of the mind. This depression of unknown origin can bring on a deadly despair. But even in this state, he says, I should remain open to the possibility that my thoughts can lead also to insight into things eternal and into future blessedness. It is helpful to know that my sad condition is uncertain and likely soon to pass away. Detachment, not indifference, should be my preferred pattern of thinking. Sorrow will always be with me. But Christ has overcome all evil, sadness, and even death itself. It is important to realize that just as I am not my thoughts, neither am I my moods and feelings. Thoughts, feelings, and moods come and go.

To stay in the middle, renunciation by controlling my thoughts is more than getting over depression or letting go of a lifestyle that is sinful. It is being aware moment by moment of the true nature of reality. In the spiritual life I need to be weaned from dependence on my physical senses in order to discover the fullness of life through my spiritual senses. Depression takes me two steps in the wrong direction. It shows me the illusory side of death and filters out a life of faith, and a life without faith destroys the dynamism pregnant in each moment and in the totality of the cosmos.

One who is afflicted with what we call chemical depression beyond the reach of ordinary spiritual practice, especially deep practices like meditation, ought to practice *faith* as much as possible. To endure this dark period can get one ready for the third renunciation, where one refrains even from attachment to one's image of God. A depressed person has a taste of what it is like to see without images, having stared into the dark abyss of nothingness. Nonetheless, even for that person there is a great gift on the other side of what we call "reality," if he stays hopeful, even in the darkness. When I experience depression, I should pray for hope, and for faith, until the darkness lifts and I can recognize beauty in the smallest trifle.

On the spiritual journey I can overcome tendencies toward gluttony, lust, grasping for things, anger, and even depression. Throughout my lifetime I will experience the long, long tedium of doing my interior work. Almost everyone who is seriously on the spiritual journey experiences a long dry period. In antiquity this "noonday devil" was called acedia.

7. About Acedia

Acedia is weariness of the soul. My heart is distressed. Dejection and anger afflict the mind; food, things, and sex burden the body; but acedia is lodged in the very soul. Hermits and desert dwellers were especially prone to this affliction. For spiritual seekers, it often occurs in the noontime of one's life, a midlife crisis. Like a fever that rises toward evening, acedia causes profound weariness.

Acedia has become identified in the popular mind as laziness of the body or sloth of the mind, and not the disease of the soul that it really is. *The New Catholic Catechism* defines *acedia* as spiritual sloth, but that, too sounds more like an attitude of one's mind and does not carry the full burden of a disease, an illness of the soul. The Catechism goes on to say that acedia goes so far as to force a person to refuse the joy that comes from God and to be repelled by divine goodness.[1]

Acedia is difficult to identify within oneself. It begins with an experience of vague uneasiness with spiritual things. My mind is sluggish and my thoughts diminish. I experience no deliberate negative thoughts at first, just a distaste for thinking of spiritual things. Soon, instead of experiencing a desire leading to thoughts (about food, sex, things), I experience a nonthought, a desire to move out of the mode of thinking at all about spiritual matters. Scriptures, readings about the saints, rituals, and pious companions seem repulsive. This

---

1. *Catechism of the Catholic Church* (Liguori, Mo.: United States Catholic Conference, Inc., 1994), #2733, 655.

nonthinking creates in me an exceptionally bad mood. It is a negative experience that shifts my soul away from any thoughts, about either evil or good. My ability to discern sleeps and is turned off and separated from reason and awareness.

It is hard to exaggerate the seriousness of acedia for a spiritual seeker. If one doesn't negotiate dejection and commits suicide out of depression, this is still only the taking of one's life out of a mental stress. Acedia, if given full sway, takes away one's inclination and merit for eternal life. It is soul-death. It has to do with our expectations of our afterlife. When one gives into acedia there is a rejection of a spiritual connection with God. It is different from ignorance, where one is listless and goes through life in a mindless way; a serious seeker has taken all the training, has achieved a certain amount of discipline through practice, and then he or she rejects a life with God.

Cassian's teaching on acedia identifies it as a secondary thought rather than just "a thought," because it is a thought about thought: Why am I doing all this? Why should I do this hard work on the spiritual journey? The psalmist refers to this thought as the "noonday devil . . . fear the terrors of night, the arrow that flies in the daytime, the plague that stalks in the dark, the scourge that wreaks havoc in broad daylight" (Ps 91:6). I hear in my head the constant refrain, What's the use? My work, my prayers, and my relationships go on as usual, but I receive no satisfaction. Time goes slowly. I am tempted to give up the religious life, interior vigilance, the spiritual journey. I often try to get others to depart from the monastery or from their own spiritual journey.

This period of life is dangerous, since all our known world is at risk: we leave marriages, monastic profession, priestly commitments, perhaps just when they are becoming beneficial to the soul. Cassian's section on the "thought of acedia" speak about the soul being sick. It is not the mind or body, but the soul that is weary of doing good, of doing anything.

This affliction is like depression, but not as dark. At first it is difficult to detect. Is this a minor case of listlessness? I might be inclined to dismiss this mood and think it is mere boredom or perhaps chronic fatigue syndrome.

The thought of acedia prompts me to desire to leave the monastery and can develop a passion to return to a self-centered life. The low energy level it creates adds to the conflict because I do not have the stamina to fight this thought. I become confused. A bad mood takes possession of me like some foul darkness. Often I regress into very superficial living, either for a short period, rebounding by God's grace, or for a protracted time, in which I may end my life without having made full efforts toward my spiritual goal. Even death just happens. The tragedy is that, under the influence of acedia, I could die while I am not really living.

Cassian's description from the monastic tradition is directed toward monks, but is instructive for all practitioners.[2] Acedia takes possession of the soul of the monk, he says. The thought of acedia produces a dislike of the place and a disgust with his cell. This disdain spreads to a contempt for the brothers who dwell with him, as if they were careless or unspiritual.

Acedia makes him lazy and sluggish about all manner of work. He imagines there is no other course except to visit either guests or other monks, or to sleep at all times day and night (*Inst.* X.3). This affliction makes him useless for every spiritual work. He no longer goes to common prayer, and no longer prays in his cell. He cannot stay in his cell nor do *lectio*.

Often he groans, saying to himself, "I can do no good if I stay here." He complains and sighs because he believes he can bear no spiritual fruit while he is joined to this community.

---

2 Cassian's, *Institutes* X, chapters 1–25, give four descriptions of a monk afflicted with acedia. I've edited the descripton.

He complains that he is cut off from spiritual gain. "I feel that I am of no use in this place." He fantasizes that if he were the abbot he would change everything, but as it is, he has no power to influence. He believes he could be more useful to a greater number of people someplace else.

He talks of a distant monastery and describes it as more profitable and better suited for his salvation. He imagines that distant community and conversations with those foreign monks as being sweet and full of the spiritual life. Cassian goes on to say that this monk is "rough." He believes that there is nothing edifying among his own community. He moans that food is scarce, and that he will never be healthy if he stays in this community. He thinks he must leave, that he will get sick and die if he stays any longer. He suggests to the abbot that he should visit sick brothers who live either near or far away. He talks about interior voices calling him to some religious duties or religious offices. He remembers a relative who needs help. He makes frequent visits with or without an invitation. He thinks to himself, "It would be a real work of piety to visit that nun (religious woman) devoted to the service of God. She is alone and without a family to support her" (*Inst.* X.2).

Acedia causes some monks to walk in a disorderly way and start meddling in other people's lives. Those afflicted with acedia are not working or walking according to the monastic tradition. They are restless and eat their bread for naught. This monk with soul-sickness decides that he can devote himself to service rather than stay useless in a cell. The only questions that remain are how to leave, where to go, and when to depart.

If he doesn't leave the monastery, he stays but merely exists. He has no energy. He is chronically fatigued. He feels hungry, weak, worn out, and tired as if he had just finished an arduous journey. Or he feels as though he has done very heavy work, or has just finished a two to three day fast (*Inst.* X.2).

Cassian continues: The afflicted monk turns this way and that and sighs. He looks for something to do with his time. If he has no visitors, he goes out and watches the sun, which is too slow in its setting. Worn out, as though by a battering ram, he sleeps. Then he flees his cell but only comes back worse than before, until he finally gives up altogether and takes flight. He not only flees the monastery, but distances himself from his very soul. Like a soldier who becomes a deserter, "he entangles himself in secular business." Cassian calls this affliction a soul-sickness. It hinders contemplation. "My soul slept from weariness." He is not body-tired; however, *his soul slept*. He has no ability to contemplate, no insight from the spiritual senses.

We see that this unfortunate monk is little by little drawn away from his cell. He begins to forget the object of his life, which is meditation and contemplation. Finally, all the interior gifts he gained by silence and prayer evaporate. This soul-sickness can be fatal, worse than suicide. The monk with this illness makes a choice to stray away from the salvation of his soul (*Inst.* X.3).

John Cassian advised his monks about what to do when plagued with the thought of acedia. If we listen carefully there is wisdom in his words for us. He told them to rededicate themselves to work in every sense. Work with your hands and be present to the work, he said, rather than dissolving into memories or thinking about desires and dreams (*Inst.* X.7). Return to the spiritual practices of common life. Check the temptation to think that you are more spiritually advanced than you really are. The benefit of the discipline may be just taking effect in you, but you consider yourself an exception and believe that the rules of the common life are beneath you. Take up your training once again by fasting, guarding your heart, manifesting your thoughts, and discerning prayerfully. Expel the desire to sleep excessively and to avoid both spiritual and physical work. Cautiously discern about running away from your ordinary routine because of some pious excuse.

The best way out of acedia, Cassian says, is to reverse all the tendencies that come from the thought. Stay in your cell, but avoid idleness and laziness. Tough out inclinations toward restlessness and traveling. Shift from an indolent manner of work to one of concentration and awareness. Refrain from visiting others out of distracted and mindless needs. Rededicate yourself to moderate refreshment and food. Be content with the work assigned. Guard against dangerous occupations.

When one is vulnerable to this affliction, it is best to avoid one who has the same affliction. Withdraw from every brother who is disorderly: those who don't make time for work, those who don't walk according to the tradition, those who are "dishonest," i.e., do not keep the proper times for going out, visiting, and talking. Beware of brothers who eat bread in great quantities. Know that silence vanishes when chatter enters. Silence includes a rule of charity. However, to break silence for the sake of assisting someone is one thing, but to break silence to keep the other from the interior life is another thing altogether. Take time to understand the one who is afflicted so that he or she will be willing to listen to advice. Abound in charity and teach by example.

Take pains to be quiet. Do your own business. Work with your own hands. Work honestly for those who are in need. Check your desires for other's possessions. Refrain from taking too much time "for yourself" because, instead of reviving energy, idle time can easily kill your industriousness, perpetuating spiritual sloth. Therefore, study and be quiet (*Inst.* XI.21).

Acedia is sometimes likened to what happens to the garment that was originally intended to give protection to your body. It has become a worn-out, moth-eaten garment. The spiritual garment given you at baptism symbolizes this protection, representing that you are clothed with the "garment of salvation." The monastic habit of the work uniform indicates the serious work you are dedicated to perform in your spiritual life. Idleness opposes such a purposeful way of life, wears out that garment, and creates many evils.

Under the cloak of idleness, interior work goes flat and dies. We lose interest in studying. Practicing silence seems pointless since nothing significant is going on, only our interior chatter with ourselves. We can see how acedia was a special problem for monks and nuns in the desert because they experienced profound stillness. They withdrew from all activities which suggested their former life to them: possessions, relationships, professions. Like present-day seekers, they became tired after a few years of difficult, persistent interior work. They were tempted to give up. Interior work, they found, is much more demanding than physical or social work. In such an environment their egos surged. No validation came from the outside for this kind of pursuit.

As a corrective, Cassian stressed the importance of creating a rhythm for work and prayer. Since idleness is the enemy of the soul, monks were charged to alternate between manual labor and pious reading. An old saying describes a monk who works as having one devil, while the monk who is idle is tormented by countless spirits. Without a rhythm between work and prayer, opportunities to give up become many and the will to go on is difficult to sustain.

Are there any benefits from overcoming the "thought of acedia"? Does Cassian's advice to the desert monks speak also to me? The feeling of no-return on my spiritual practices separates my *intention* out from my action. The chief benefit of facing acedia can be to purify my motivation. It can cause me for the first time to start doing spiritual practices for the right reasons rather than for subtle self-gain. It is not enough to do the right thing, even if we are engaged in charitable works. A genuine seeker must do the right things for the right reasons.

A second by-product of overcoming acedia is that manual labor itself becomes a spiritual practice. John Cassian advised the desert monks to do manual labor in order to disperse the stale energies of acedia. He assured them that by doing so, they would experience the joy of manual labor. Therefore, he advised the monks to work as they prayed and to pray without ceasing. Surrender wholeheartedly to the will of God, he said. Suffer patiently. Practice humility and obedience.

Sometimes, when a practitioner has long been in training for spiritual things—practicing fasting, detachment from things, chaste thoughts, discernment, and moderation—the soul becomes weary. There is a surge of the self that wants to compete for control of our most inner thoughts. To pray without ceasing is a labor. The sweetness of spiritual consolations wears off. There is no apparent return for all one's effort. In short, the seeker is tired of the spiritual journey. Monastics would say that manual labor breaks through consciousness, gives one initial distance from spiritual practices, frees the mind from thinking, so that unthinking can occur. The mind clears and becomes pure. Manual labor done mindfully is wonderful for redirecting motivation.

But what if my work is all mental and I don't have the luxury of doing manual work? The danger to the soul in intellectual overstimulation is to be taken seriously. The teachings on acedia prompt me to take some corrective measures in order to move into routine, repetitive work. Gardening, sewing, carpentry, or cooking can take on a new purpose: to lead me to a state of unthinking. My ordinary work of cleaning, bathing, washing clothes, restoring order in my workplace can help. Walking, driving, and routine physical exercise can benefit my soul as well as my body.

The trick is what I do with my mind—my thoughts—when I do such maintenance work. When I walk, preferably outside, I should let my thoughts come and then let them go. When I do this, ceaseless prayer begins to rise. On the conscious level I'm not thinking about anything. I am mindful only insofar as I am not mindful of anything in particular. My mind is alert, awake, receiving. The more I can refrain from particular thoughts, the more my other layers of consciousness surface.

Taciturnity is a technical term from antiquity. It means to refrain from speaking for the sake of the work going on in one's interior life (*RB* 6). The practice of taciturnity is to refrain from saying even good things to good people. The purpose of this practice is to train the mind to think twice before speaking. This kind of silence schools the "thinker" in unthinking. When I'm not supposed to have an opinion on everyone and everything, the mind slowly learns to rest, receive, observe, and listen.

Bodily work relieves pressures on the mind. Since the major symptom of the malady of acedia is that I am not able to pray anymore, work with my hands may help me be productive until my mind returns to concentration. My body restores rest to my overactive mind, and returns them to balance. Work is a back door to pure prayer. For a proficient practitioner, who is working mindfully, there is no distinction between work and prayer. Prayer is work and work is prayer. The right motivation accompanies the right action. I remember a sister at Beech Grove who had been working in the kitchen announced at the dinner table, "Today I learned that the kitchen is not about food, but charity."

Our desert teacher, Cassian, observed the monks working: some had a one-thing-at-a-time rhythm, moving with grace and poise through tedious, repetitive tasks. Other monks were fighting the "work" and resisting each motion. It seems as though the first group of monks worked from the center of their heart and the second worked from wild swings of random thoughts coming from here and there taking the monk away from the sacredness of the moment. To be mindful is a safe harbor; a ship is anchored, the water stilled (*Inst.* II.14).

Perhaps the finest teachings about apostolic work are in the section devoted to avoiding the thought of acedia. In that section, John Cassian advised his monks that preaching, teaching, and healing should not replace the mandate to serve through manual labor. We become restless, he says, if we are not content to work with our hands. We who preach the gospel ought to live the gospel. We should not eat by collections and gifts, but from labor and weariness. We should work night and day and be supported by our own labor. Here again the directive is to be diligent in supplying our needs not from our store of abundance or from money laid up or from another's generosity, but rather through the sum of our own labor and toil.

What kind of work should be done by a serious seeker? This list comes from the fourth century: We should do the interior work of patience and humility. We should refresh pilgrims by hospitality or visit prisoners. We should remember to give to the poor who are suffering from famine and barrenness and should offer reasonable and true sacrifice. Notice that the apostolic work mentioned here is not directed toward family and friends. Though they must not be excluded, the rule of thumb is to give to those who cannot give in return, to move into selfless service, to imitate the sacrifice of Jesus.

This becomes a double grace, giving as Christ and receiving as Christ. Mother Teresa of Calcutta often reiterated this theme: to serve as Christ and to receive the poor who reveal Christ to us. The worst thing a practitioner can do is to give out of pretense. The source of giving must be our own labor, not money secured through avarice and greed. Charity, to be pure, must be produced by our own toil. This kind of work has an intimate quality that acts out matters of faith in daily life.

Are there any benefits to thought of acedia"? Perhaps the greatest benefit is that the meaning of true leisure emerges. Leisure is not the same as idleness. What spiritual seekers look for in leisure is not idleness but meaning and an experience of purity that enables us to transcend ordinary consciousness. When I have removed the obstacles of acedia, then prayer and work return without the drag of negative attitudes toward work. Leisure in manual labor, study, or prayer is possible for the first time. The tradition teaches that the fruit of acedia is such leisure. When I am one with myself, stilled in thought, having no anxiety in my body, and fully attentive to what I am doing, leisure, work, and prayer are all the same. Purity of heart happens.

How shall we act toward someone with acedia? Kindness is to be shown to the sick. Acedia is an illness and it is important to be kind to anyone with illness of body or mind. But just because someone else is sick, we should not become ill ourselves. We need to refrain from joining the listless person or absorbing the climate of laziness of this person who is ill. We need to redouble our own zeal and demonstrate compassion to the afflicted person. Cassian advises that we are to be kind even if the afflicted one has ignored or rebuffed our attempts to help. If we don't show charity toward those with the illness of acedia, then we will be guilty of the same vice. Do good, encourage the afflicted one by words of consolation and by words of correction.

Should we discipline one with acedia? The fathers advise us to admonish not out of hatred, but out of love. This person is not an enemy, but a brother or sister, and we should combine the affection of a parent with the severity of a judge. Temper with kindness and gentleness the sentence you deliver with apostolic sternness, he says. Yet Cassian warns us not to keep his or her company. Our affection and hope for change, he says, sometimes necessitate excommunication of the affected person. Such isolation will restore him or her to the way of salvation (*Inst.* X.15). Remember that all of us need to support the weak, but this must be done in such a way that we nonetheless have a safety net of support. St. Benedict sends a *senpectae*—a wise brother—to extend support while the community and the abbot stand firm with the boundaries (*RB* 27:2). What is interesting about "cutting off" the erring member, is that in acedia the seeker is tepid and wants to leave anyway. To move him out against his will may destroy the illusion that the group is not worthy of his talents, this may have the effect of reawakening the afflicted one, causing him to return to his commitments.

The Rule of Benedict articulates a strong sense of group. It was a privilege to belong to the monastery. The individual was reverenced, but the group was a partner in the dialogue about membership. A caring group set boundaries that assisted others to make healthy choices. Sometimes an individual might discern that he must be away from the group, and that was healthy, too. Boundaries gave a starting point for dialogue. The thought of acedia, however, creates a desire to move away from the group because the spiritual discipline is too demanding. A monk afflicted with acedia might persuade another to leave, e.g., a senior monk might tell a novice monk that he "needs a companion," and the novice may leave and the senior stay. Abbot Moses counseled Brother Paul: "You fled, but the next attack will be worse. Stay and don't sleep. Resist it. Stay" (*Inst.* X.25).

How should I "stay?" What do I do in my cell? What and where is a cell for a lay person? A cell is a technical term in the monastic tradition.[3] According to Thomas Merton, the right

---

3. Thomas Merton, *Contemplation in a World of Action* (New York: Doubleday, 1997), 252–59.

order of things in the solitary life is this: everything is centered on union with God in prayer and solitude. Therefore, the most important ascetic practice is solitude itself, and "sitting" alone in the silence of the cell. It is more than a bedroom or a place to sleep. It is the equivalent of each monastic's personal space for being alone before God. This space is sacred, and is usually not shared under any circumstances, not for the sake of being alone, but for the sake of being with God. My sisters have taught me seven functions of a contemplative's cell:

- It is the place that is also the teacher because it is where we memorize the psalms, Scripture, and other sacred texts. Part of the early formation for Benedictine monks and nuns was to memorize the seventy-three chapters of *The Rule of Benedict*. When you have that rule in your heart and have memorized it in that cell, the walls talk to you when you are deliberating, sorting your thoughts.

- It is the place to practice recollection, to do *lectio divina*, Centering Prayer, sitting meditation, and to pray without ceasing. It is a place of rest where one refrains from working. In the section on pure prayer, Cassian says that overworking is the biggest obstacle to seekers moving into the kind of prayer that is an absorption into God, beyond images (*Conf.* IX). This overwork, especially in the monastery, is manifested by excess. It is a spiritual drunkenness. The cell is deliberately simple, so there is little care and possibility of overworking working.

- It is a place for listening. A benefit of routine is that the mind and soul get into a rhythm. The nervous system shifts into a lower gear. Rest happens, and a deeper listening from the heart is restored. The monastic term *horarium* refers to this rhythm. Each day, each week, and each season has natural cycles with which to be in tune.

- It is a place of truth. I can actually see how many possessions I have, how few things I need, and how my thoughts come and how they go. It is a place where I actually experience that I am not my thoughts.

- It is a personal sanctuary. This safe place holds me secure in my resolve and moves me in the direction of my commitments, even when I feel no zeal.
- It reminds me daily that time is fleeting. I will soon die. Death happens to me personally, and it is something that I must do alone. There is no running from my cell, or my death.
- It is a place to sleep, to surrender, to experience the night. The cell cannot be stressed enough in the formation of beginners. Sleeping and waking governs one's day. For spiritual practitioners, that sacred space it a place of working out this wholehearted pursuit.

But what if I am married and share my bedroom? Marriage is precisely the arrangement where individuals do all of the above, together. In the case of death, I promise to accompany the other until the last breath. All the functions of a cell can be carried out in the sacred bedroom of a couple committed to each other in the holy vows of marriage.

But what if I don't have a partner who is on the spiritual journey? It is difficult to be married to a partner who is on another path. It is very hard to be in a religious community or in the priesthood if the interior work is not recognized nor valued. But if one has heard the voice calling him or her to this contemplative path, there is no way to stop those desires . . . and the heart will find a way. The original idea of Abba Anthony was to go it alone. Perhaps such a solo is your radical calling. A cell is a place to cry, alone and for reasons of the heart that you don't have to explain to anyone else. The teachings on acedia speak of these moments that can last for years.

Acedia creates a dried-up soul. Tears soften us and prepare us to begin again, as if in our first fervor. We find the teaching

on tears in the practice of compunction of heart (*penthos*).[1]
"Compunction," says the *Philokalia,* is the state of one who is
"pricked to the heart, who has become conscious of his distance from God; who has a mingled feeling of sorrow, tender-
ness, and joy, springing from sincere repentance"(428). Acedia
is a soul-sickness, a loss of any connection with spiritual things.
Practices mean nothing. Boredom is too weak a word. Perhaps
aversion or repulsion regarding the spiritual dimensions of life
and living better describe the effects of acedia.

Compunction, however, is a felt experience of being
struck down, pierced to the heart. One is moved to deep sorrow and repentance. Compunction isn't something that happens to a seeker once or twice, after some sinful incident.
Compunction is a burning state, like being in love. It is a
resolve, a heightened relationship with God that seems not to
have moods or periods of doubt. When we feel compunction,
we feel like a sinner in constant need of God's mercy.

The tradition maintains that the "fear of God is the
beginning of wisdom." Compunction leads us to the kind of
fear that makes sense. Not a neurotic fear created by the ego,
but a fear that leads to a right relationship with God. Humility
is a right relationship with myself; fear is a right relationship
with God. Humility is particularly fitting for those of us working on the second renunciation where we remove all obstacles
between us and God.

Compunction causes an impulse in us to come closer,
through remorse, to love and union with God, not hiding in
shame or guilt. Remorse purifies. The naked self stands before
God. Pierced to the heart, the seeker experiences an overwhelming sense of the importance of a relationship with God.
Separation, wrongdoing, lazy thinking, and a sluggish heart

---

4. Irenee Hausherr, S.J., *Penthos: The Doctrine of Compunction in the
Christian East* (Kalamazoo, Mich.: Cistercian Publications, Inc., 1987), 52.

are inappropriate ways to approach the object of love. Once more, dualistic language helps to remind the earnest soul that he or she has not yet arrived at the stage of unity. There is distance between the soul and God. God calls, beacons, and attracts the seeker with major consolations.

The good news is that true sorrow for wrongdoing and consent to God's forgiveness are sufficient to cancel all the negative attachment to guilt. God's forgiveness means just that. *All* is forgiven. Through faith we let go of the event and the memory of the event. Once again, in an instant, we enjoy a relationship of favor with God.

To obsess on past negative actions shows a lack of faith in God. It doesn't matter who was wrong: myself, my parents, teachers, authorities. It is over. As thoughts rise, the believer prays once again with wholehearted faith. If feelings of dejection linger, they are only thoughts. If attachment to negative feelings dominate one's consciousness, this is not compunction; it is a lack of faith in God's great goodness. Christ asks us to put our head on his heart and let him carry our burdens. Honest remorse takes away any trace of wrongdoing. This news is so good that we have a hard time enjoying it.

Compunction of heart is an abiding gift of consciousness that is not only an inward disposition, but is a real emotional state, often accompanied by tears. These tears come at night, at daybreak, at prayer, at work, and during stillness.

How is compunction different from depression? Depression is something to get over, as is acedia. Compunction is the awakening of a dead heart and the experience of a right relationship with God. There is no sadness in the "gift of tears," only gratefulness for being forgiven, being alive, being in relationship with God. The sorrow of compunction is a wholesome sorrow, knowing the hard times are over, and the past is past. Remembrance is consoling, a celebration of having come home.

Is compunction a remembrance of sin? No. What

thoughts are appropriate to one who has been awakened from hardness of heart and now has the gift of tears? Tears become the prayer. When we experience tears, we refrain from analysis of childhood, from significant relationships, from traumatic episodes. The past does not exist and never did. When tears come, I should let them flow unaccompanied by commentary. Tears are the language of the soul. Words are the language of the mind. When I am silently crying in my heart, I take more time for silence, vigils, and prayer. When tears come, I breathe deeply and rest. I know I am swimming in a hallowed stream where many have gone before. I am not alone, crazy, or having a nervous breakdown. This is sweet sorrow. My heart is at work. My soul is awake.

Is acedia the same thing as the dark night of the senses, or the "dark night of the soul"? St. John of the Cross lived a thousand years after John Cassian and he came from a different philosophical system of thought. One point of connection from both traditions, however, is that both acedia and the dark nights have as a benefit a purification of our motivations; they both move the seeker on the spiritual journey. But acedia and "dark nights" differ somewhat in the way they are manifested according to their descriptions.

Acedia comes at midlife, whereas dark nights occur only after achieving a refined, delicate, deep relationship with God in the interior life. Dark nights are trials of those already spiritually proficient. Acedia occurs to those making the second renunciation, the renunciation of thoughts. Those experiencing dark nights are making the third renunciation, letting go of their thoughts and images of God. For this reason, it seems preferable to relate acedia to the experience of spiritual sloth. Dark nights are the trials of the spiritually more advanced.

Perhaps I should make a clarification here. Thoughts cycle through our lives time and time again, but there is a gradation among them. Explaining this gradation is the genius of

Cassian's and Evagrius's teaching on thoughts. The three classic states of the soul are purgative, illuminative, and unitive. The second renunciation belongs to the purgative stage. From the point of view of Origen, one has not begun the spiritual journey until one has renounced one's former (exterior) life. Then the interior journey has three phases: purgative, illuminative, and unitive. The dark nights that John of the Cross so aptly describes is the purification of the illuminative stage wherein the soul is moving toward union or the completion of the third renunciation of letting go even the thought of God. We know little about these later stages because anyone having arrived would not talk about it! They'd be "silent in the Presence," as Abhishiktananda reports.[5]

The affliction of the "thought of acedia" prompts me to leave the path of the interior journey toward God. In fact, if I fail to move through the thoughts of food, sex, things, anger, and dejection, I may never even experience acedia, since if I am not doing soul-work I will not have any weariness of the soul.

As we advance on the spiritual journey, our training gets more and more advanced. If we stay on the course, we must learn harder and harder lessons. The "thought of vainglory" is a pernicious one. It is the next affliction that moves against the advancing practitioner.

---

5. *Swami Abhishiktananda*, ed. James Stuart (Delhi, India: ISPACK, 1995), 266. He writes in 1972, "Just now I am rereading John of the Cross and Teresa of Ávila. I can make out what they are saying, but how strange and complicated is their 'language'—like Chinese to a European. Once the language of the Upanishad is freed from its ritual-magic substratum, what purity and directness it has by contrast" (271).

8. About Vainglory

The seventh thought is "about vainglory," taking credit for good actions. *Glory* means God's presence, the very life of God in my soul. How does John Cassian define *vainglory*? He says it is doing the right thing for the wrong reason. The reasons usually have to do with puffing up the self, becoming something other than one's true being. Further, Cassian says it is difficult to detect vainglory in someone else because he or she looks so perfect, and it is almost impossible to notice it in myself since I am generally under a cloud of self-delusion. Vainglory is related to my motivation. Like acedia, which brings to my awareness thoughts about what I am thinking and doing, vainglory is also called a secondary thought. It is not about something that I do, but about what I am thinking when I do it. The word *vain* relates to nothingness, illusion, emptiness. The self takes credit for what it didn't do! *Vainglory* refers to what others think, how I am perceived. I actually perceive myself through what I think others think of me.

Many spiritual directors can't detect this affliction. Cassian emphasizes that inexperienced directors may inadvertently feed our ego instead of leading us through and out of this affliction, as they would with thoughts about sex, food, or things. Consequently, we become more self-deceived, thinking that we are enlightened and holy. We even begin to be leaders and become even more dangerous to ourselves and others. Self-delusion abounds and followers can be led astray, also.

Vainglory is the opposite of dejection. These two afflictions are the reverse sides of the same coin. In dejection, I put myself down; in vainglory I place myself above. The practice of humility is to be neither too high nor too low. The practice of right thinking is to attribute to God's goodness any glory I see in myself. To be grateful is fitting and proper. But if, under the influence of self-delusion I become overconfident, I then become vain. Vainglory is called presumption when I act out on the assumption that I'm better than someone else. If I entertain vain thoughts about my own abilities and put myself ahead of others, eventually I lose any sense of discrimination. I no longer can distinguish the grace of God from my own efforts.

While the human soul enlivens both the body and the mind, the Holy Spirit enlivens the soul, the dwelling place of God. Therefore, to take credit for the good in my soul is to usurp the presence of the Holy Spirit. The "thought of vainglory" is self-reflexive interior chatter. I take credit for all the good the self does. I think grand thoughts about myself. Vainglory replaces God with the self as one's object of worship.

It is impossible to exaggerate the importance of the word *glory* in antiquity. Bruno Barnhardt, O.S.B. Cam., reminds us that when Jesus said that he was the glory of God, he meant that he fully embodied God as man. When he invited us to share that life, he invited us to enter into God's glory. Language fails to communicate how important this invitation to all of us is. Glory is the experienced presence of God. This manifestation is perceptible, whether in the cloud that filled the tabernacle in the desert, or in the pillar of fire that guided the Israelites through the desert, or as a person in the temple. Barnhardt goes on to say that this glory is a concrete reality, an appearance, a palpable presence. God submits to human experience and at the same time overwhelms it. The work of Jesus—from his incarnation to his death and resurrection—is to bring humanity into the glory of God, or, conversely, to bring divine glory into the human body, to make divine glory immanent in creation.

Glory, he says, is the song which sings from the words of
the Gospel; it is the flame that springs up within me when the
word touches my heart. And it is God—excess, pure gratuity,
transcendent in being, more intimate to me than my own
hungry and struggling self. Glory is that which glows at the
extremes of experience: at the heights and the depths of life.
Everything in the world moves toward glory as its flowering,
its coming to flame, its truth. Shame is the inverse of glory, a
terrible knowledge of our destiny, the awful nakedness we feel
without the garment of light. Beauty is the icon of glory, the
light of eternity on the features of time.[1]

Without a sense of adoration and reverence, the word
glory loses its power to communicate a sense of God in one's
interior life. If I am afflicted with vainglory, I take to myself
what is proper to God, namely glory. If I take to myself what
belongs to God, I am vain. This affliction attacks the spiritual side of serious seekers, afflicts those who have already
demonstrated that they can't be deceived by carnal vices.
Vainglory is a wound of the spiritually proficient. Subtly, ever
so slightly, under the influence of this seventh thought, I twist
the truth in order to move toward self instead of toward God.

John Cassian describes the experience of the "thought of
vainglory" in those seeking God. To have spent years practicing all the virtues and then to start attributing our good life to
our own doing as if we didn't need God anymore, he says, spiritually endangers a person in pursuit of purity of heart. Under
the influence of *apatheia*, the thoughts are stilled and God
emerges. If in the stilled heart the self rises instead of God,
however, spiritual powers of keen insight and single-minded
concentration can look good, but be brutally devastating.

---

1. Bruno Barnhardt, *The Good Wine* (Mahway, N.J.: Paulist Press,
1993), 99–101.

Pride, when I start doing the wrong things for the wrong reason, is the end stage. But pride begins with vainglory when, while still doing the right things for the wrong reasons, I begin to appropriate to myself what belongs to God.

Vainglory can take many exterior forms: dress, manner, walk, voice, work, vigils, fasts, prayers, reading. It also can take many interior forms: silence, obedience, humility, patience. The self-delusion of vainglory is like a dangerous rock hidden just beneath the water. It will wreck the ship if the pilot does not stay on guard. Vainglory attacks just after I have achieved a sense that I have made the virtues a lifestyle. It is an illness coming from both the right (good impulses) and the left (negative impulses). It comes from the right because I flatter myself about my perfect practice. It attacks the left because I end up glorying in my shame. "No one is as bad as I am." To be the worst sinner is to glory in one's wicked ways, to be more worthy than anyone else of God's forgiveness. Either way, such vainglory puffs up the ego.

Vainglory is very subtle. In the case of food, I begin to think that my fasting is better than anyone else's, even my moderation in eating and drinking is a better moderation than anyone else's middle way. Extreme thinking, either positive or negative, is a clue that I am afflicted with this thought. If I am very good at spiritual practice and take credit for my virtue, this is vainglory. I can even be so deceived that I take honor in having great humility. I can show off my knowledge in an elegant way, or demonstrate the practice of silence by a protracted heavy weight of solemnity that tries to be better than anyone else's silence. Even fasting can be a source of pride. This "I can do anything" attitude is dangerous to the soul. To refuse honor, to be self-effacing, may also be a mark of vainglory. Though done for the right reasons this is not indifference, but humility.

Mother Teresa illustrated humility, not vainglory. She met with the rich and famous, never apologized for her presence, but spoke of being a pencil, an instrument for God's work. She never took credit *toward herself* and certainly not *for herself*.

Cassian described how vainglory can manipulate even a sincere seeker: So as not to fall into vainglory, he avoids long prayers in front of others, yet his motivation in doing this is haughty (*Inst.* XI.4). Many saints recount that they actually interrupted their spiritual practices, because if they were observed by someone else, they might receive praise and that praise would go to their heads. So they felt it would be better not to do these practices, because such actions could turn into a vice, a perverse form of virtue, due to the possibility of vainglory.

But Cassian sees this kind of thinking as a trick, encouraging one to resist legitimate spiritual practices, with the excuse that it isn't really good for the soul to be good at them. As one progresses in the spiritual journey, discernment is absolutely necessary because good things look bad and bad things look good. Cassian recommended that discussing the problem with a seasoned elder could help the sorting process.

Vainglory can penetrate all the gains I have obtained through spiritual practice. This thought can't be conquered by solitude. It pursues me and puffs me up because of my endurance of work and labor in an exemplary way. My extreme readiness to obey causes me to outstrip others in humility, knowledge, reading, and vigils. Spiritual greed brings me high praise.

This vice winds through all the virtues. All along the path, I walk elated by success, impressed with my greatness. My triumphs and my overstraining of the limits of self-restraint cause me to fail. I run so hard and become so uptight, I begin to set impossible goals. I have escalated my austerities to a crisis of limits. I fall. Then I stop all practices. Or if I keep practicing, I am in danger of success. The more I practice, the worse it gets. Even with diligent practice in the spiritual life more temptations can be generated, food for the eager thought of vainglory. If I overcome vainglory once, then the temptation gets keener. If I overcome vainglory temporarily, but then celebrate my success as my own victory, I dig deeper into this insidious affliction.

Cassian says that being older and more mature is no help either. In my advancing years, even if I am still living a life in the desert, the thought of vainglory can penetrate all barriers, encouraged by the achievement of virtues. It is skillful, diligent, and feeds on success, which then provides more fuel for vanity. Because vainglory is mixed up with the virtues, it is more dangerous. It comes in the cloak of night. I am caught off guard. Success and prosperity are dangerous. Under the influence of vainglory, I become so confident that I ignore the three guides that were so helpful in the past: my teachers, the Scriptures, and my experience. Under the influence of self-delusion, I ignore all three guides, adhering instead to what the ego desires and considers important. Spiritual things are ineffectual if the teacher is commending what he or she has no experience of, and is trying with empty-sounding words to instruct his or her hearer, or else the hearer is a person full of faults and cannot receive in his or her hard heart the holy and saving teachings of the spiritual teacher (*Conf.* XIV.18).

The mind takes great leaps. I can do this or that, because I feel called to assist this person or that. Presumption takes my desires further and further. An end-stage symptom emerges when I think I have already done what still needs to be done in the spiritual life. "I don't need fasting, prayers, or the practices anymore." I set myself on a higher level than the one to which my soul has evolved. "Do not aspire to be called holy before you really are, but first be holy that you may more truly be called so" (*RB* 4. 62).

One can be afflicted with vainglory in private or in community. If one prefers aloneness, there is no opportunity for being puffed up with vanity that comes from outside comments. However, if one is living with others, there are more occasions to become vain.

John Cassian warned monks about some of the most common ways that vainglory might hook them: I have a good voice so I can sing better than others. My body is either emaciated and looks more ascetic than others, or I have a good figure that commands notice. I might be from a rich family but I have renounced the good life, or I deserve special consideration because my family was the poorest of the poor. Or I inflate myself with imaginary greatness by telling myself that if only I had stayed in the world I would have had everything, or that in a few years I will be ordained a priest and will be successful at winning souls.

Cassian taught that through daydreaming one can see himself teaching and preaching and receiving standing ovations with wild applause. Vainglory intoxicates the mind. It resembles a profound slumber, a sensuous daydream. I am really somewhere that does not exist, but I am missing the present. I dwell with my wandering thoughts and walk in my dreams, as if they were true.

Vainglory sometimes takes the form of envy. I see in others what I think I deserve myself. I desire another's good looks, great voice, keen mind, and accomplishments with such force that I can taste it. I fantasize that I am actually that other person. Or I become angry with them because they have the gifts I want. I take to myself what glory properly belongs to another, rather than thanking God for the gifts I see in others.

What is the cure for vainglory? Cassian advised the monks to discover the root causes and lay bare their innermost thoughts. He again prescribed the practice of manifestation of thoughts (*exagoreusis*): when one lays his thoughts out to a wise one, those thoughts can be obliterated. Through spiritual conferences with a wise elder, one can learn how to prevent the thoughts of vainglory from gaining a foothold.

Root out the motive of self-glory, especially in its subtle shapes. Maintain yourself with solemn care and watch for the signs of vainglory. They can be detected by observing yourself boasting, being competitive, telling remarkable tales about yourself, seeking the credit, or taking on yourself the role of the hero. Cassian goes on to say that the cure for vainglory can start very early in the spiritual life. Through watchfulness of thoughts, I can edit, redirect, and change thoughts about myself that are either high (praise) or low (dejection). The practice of humility encourages me to think about myself exactly as I am.

Watchfulness or vigilance over my thoughts is a specific practice that will anticipate situations or inklings that engender either grandiose thoughts (vainglory), or low-self-esteem thoughts (dejection). Guard of the heart is a practice that will anticipate those thoughts and lead to prayer. Prayer is a barrier to unwelcome thoughts. Return to ceaseless prayer. There are times when one cannot meditate, because of the pressures of life, but we are all called to prayer without ceasing. When prayer is automatically going on in the heart, vainglory cannot exist.

Cassian taught that there may be benefits to an awareness of the thought of vainglory. The first benefit is the fruit of discernment for service (*Inst.* XI.14). If I overcome the thought of vainglory, then I am fully ready to take on the role of ministry. I serve, not for the sake of self gain, but for the sake of the people and their needs. If I have overcome the tendency to vainglory, I can discern what God is really calling me to do. If it is manual labor, fine. If it is teaching, preaching, or healing, fine. If it is to be a leader like an abbot, priest, or pastoral minister, fine. The seeker can follow the will of God confidently, knowing his work is not just a means to greater esteem from others.

Second, I can overcome embarrassment that either comes from praise or shame. Since I am looking for neither response, and am only doing things for the honor and glory of God, an interior spiritual poise develops. I can move with rich or poor, the common or the famous, friends or enemies. There is no difference. The fruit is equanimity.

Third, I realize that watching my thoughts, either when I am alone or with others, is liberating. When my motivation is the honor and glory of God and not my own aggrandizement, it makes no difference if I practice alone, or with others. The discipline of the thoughts is the same, whether I am in the monastery, in a family setting, or at a community function. While overcoming acedia trains the mind to *do*, using manual labor or prayer interchangeably, overcoming vainglory trains the person to *live* the spiritual life either alone or with others. The cell is the place for watching over my thoughts (*Conf.* VI.15). If I can do that same interior practice in the midst of a crowd, there is no need for the desert. So while a solitary life is helpful to know my thoughts, the practice of watchfulness can be a mental substitute for the desert culture of a monk or a hermit.

When I have overcome vainglory, my sense of self is true and right. What today's seekers desire when they try to improve their self-esteem is actually the fruit of overcoming vainglory and dejection. I obtain a sense of self in harmony with my grace and nature. There is nothing lacking, according to my ego. I feel balanced and stilled. The glory of God is present, my spiritual senses are awakened and illuminations (seeing things clearly for the first time, or being bathed in great light) begin to happen in prayer. There is no competition for attention. I experience profound moments of oneness.

But what if these practices to reduce vainglory also reduce my confidence in myself? The practices that move out vainglory will not displace self confidence, but will rather place the good action, thought, or motivation in the light of God's goodness, not my own. What is most compelling about the practice of the thoughts is the strong directives they pre-scribe. If I lay aside my own thoughts, grace emerges and provides me strength for the good life. There need be no striv-ing for virtue. The practice of laying aside thoughts uncovers divine grace, the glory of God, whose energy takes over. Charity springs up (*Inst.* IV.43).

There is no corresponding list of eight virtues to replace the eight thoughts. Lay aside one's thoughts and all the virtues emerge. I cannot pull out a spiritual repertoire to indicate what response is needed. When I live with a discerning heart, there are no causes or right actions that tell me what to do. I simply have a loving heart, ready to do whatever is necessary. I don't dwell on outside causes. I lead a life close to the heart and am guided by whispers.

What if I feel dejected, and see no good in myself or oth-ers? Isn't vainglory good for self-esteem? Cassian has addressed the issue of self-esteem in previous chapters. It is important to re-emphasize his teaching about self-esteem, particularly not-ing the link between vainglory and dejection.

To feel bad about myself is a form of pride. What I am really telling myself is that I am the worst of the worst: no one exceeds me in unworthiness. The right attitude before God, however, is humility. I am not perfect and I am in need of God's grace. Why should I feel good about myself? Or why should I feel bad about myself? It is all the same. I am. Thoughts, feelings, passions come and go. Thoughts not entertained move out. There are no promises on the spiritual journey that good actions beget good feelings about the self, especially if I keep putting my expectations higher and high-er. If I do so, I will always feel dejected. The root of my dejec-tion is not that I have poor self-esteem, but that I place myself above what is. Humility is hard work in the spiritual journey. This truth will be even more evident when we study John Cassian's teachings on pride.

What if I have done something extraordinary, even great? Can't I enjoy that? Cassian advises that joy that is rich and full is from the fruits of virtuous action. Thoughts are neither good nor bad; they just are. The problem with elation and dejection is that what often looks good, is not good. The things that seem bad are often quite beneficial. So to rise and fall emotionally on what is perceived as good and bad is vain. The practice is to give glory to God and to be grateful in everything. The practice of compunction (*penthos*) produces a profound fruit that gives all glory to God and asks for mercy for one's self.

So are we saying that good self-esteem is really vainglory? Isn't that life denying? Can't that kind of thinking lead to neurotic patterns? Cassian emphasizes that self-esteem doesn't exist. The self, the ego, reports reality as it *seems*. The self-esteem journey looks like this: I've been wounded and I feel alienated, hurt, and abused. I need help, comfort, security, and healing. This will take some time so I'll need more time for myself to work on my body, my feelings, and my intellect. Doesn't anyone care about me, about what I do and who I am? I need intimacy and the comfort of others who really understand me from the inside and know where I've been. I'll never be a victim again. Does anyone hear the depths of my pain? When I'm with others I feel that I need to be alone, but when I'm alone I feel lonely and need to be with others. I need to have less work and responsibility while I am going through all this emotional turmoil. I'll help others when I get it together.

On the contrary, the train of thought for those seeking God moves in the opposite direction: I kneel before God in awe and adoration. I take off my shoes. My nakedness is all that I have to offer. Listening with the ear of my heart, I follow the impulse of grace to move away from attachments that linger in my consciousness. But I'm also drawn toward joy and song. My steps quicken toward all I love. If I discern that it is the will of my Beloved, I'm ready to lay down my life for another.

To get from the first set of dialogues toward the self to the second set of dialogues away from the self and toward God and others, we have to practice the simple, but difficult work of dealing with our thoughts: guard of the heart, watchfulness over the thoughts, anticipating difficulties rather than responding to them, vigilance.

To participate in the grace of God and all the promises of the Holy Spirit is to become fully alive. The gifts that come to one who is listening, open, and willing, penetrate the heart, quicken the mind, and incite the body with life beyond the ordinary. To be seeking self-esteem rather than an all-out pursuit of God is contrary to the spiritual life.

In summary, vainglory can be prevented by the practice of watchfulness and prayer. Vigilance of thought and guard of the heart anticipate the thought of vainglory and its commentaries. This watchfulness is an interior practice of noticing not only what I am thinking, desiring, and doing, but also *how* I am thinking about the thoughts, about the desires, and about the deeds. Watchfulness steps up its guard. Compunction of heart reminds me of my longing for God and my need to stay faithful to the practices of the spiritual journey.

The first layer of thoughts was about food, sex, things, anger, and depression. The second layer is thoughts about the thought of those things, about motivation, purpose, meaning, and intention. Literally, the practice in thoughts about acedia and vainglory is to be attentive to one's intention. The intention of the spiritual life is to move away from the deluded self and toward God. In return, a deep relationship with God emerges. In *Inst.* IV, Cassian makes this summary: We can mount up to the heights of perfection without difficulty. "The beginning of salvation and of wisdom is," according to Scripture, "the fear of the Lord" (Ps 111:3). From the fear of the Lord arises compunction. From compunction of heart springs renunciation, nakedness, and detachment from possessions. From nakedness comes humility and the relinquishment of desires. Through relinquishment of desires all faults are removed; virtues shoot up and increase. By the budding of virtues, purity of heart happens. With purity of heart, the perfection of apostolic love is acquired. This sequence of activities suggests that if we use effort to remove obstacles to grace, the virtuous life rises spontaneously with full energy, reaching out in loving compassion.

It is important for me to know the interior practices that Cassian describes, so that I can remove obstacles to them. It is essential to be vigilant, to keep up the practice of ceaseless prayer. Through watchfulness I move once again into prayer without ceasing because this practice silences the internal chatter that tempts me to take credit for the success of my spiritual, intellectual, or physical work. "Watch and pray," is what Jesus said to his disciples at the end of his earthly ministry when they went to the garden of Gethsemane. If I consent to vainglory and take credit for my good actions, all the forces of pride emerge. Pride is without a doubt the most dangerous of all the thoughts.

We have seen how food, sex, and things pertain to the body; how anger and dejection afflict the mind; and how acedia, vainglory, and now pride are spiritual sicknesses of the soul. The soul can be either an individual or a social soul, as in the soul of a group or nation. In the case of the three thoughts that pertain to the soul—acedia, vainglory, and pride—we must control these in order for the very soul to be released from bondage. Of these three, pride is dangerously close to wanting to be like God, determining what the good is for others. Successful people that have negotiated years of spiritual training find pride the most difficult "of thoughts."

9. About Pride

Pride is the most deadly of all the thoughts because it tries to conquer the perfect. Pride poisons all of my previous work regarding thoughts, all my desires and passions. When I am doing all the right things with regard to food, sex, anger, things, dejection, and acedia, I begin to feel that I can accomplish everything on my own (vainglory). With only a slight jump I can then imagine that I am the engineer of my own destiny, and I can determine the destiny of others, too.

Cassian describes the process this kind of thinking: I begin to think that things that would be wrong for another to do are permissible for me, since I am so good. I think I know what is good for myself and for others. I drop all the monastic and spiritual practices because I am above the law. I can't benefit from prayers, fasting, rules of poverty, chastity and obedience anymore. There is no one to be obedient to, since I know best. Vainglory has to do with what others think and my own perception of that governs what I do, but pride has to do with my very being. Pride is who I am.

The description John Cassian paints of a person full of pride is classic: We see a monk strutting, talking loudly, laughing raucously, tapping his fingers on the table while another is speaking, carrying his body haughtily, with no recollection of the inner life, since his thoughts, actions and passions are all justifiable. This person makes judgments about what is good for everyone around him. Often this monk is in leadership and dominates. His will is Godlike. He makes another do wrong to serve him. No one can tell him anything. Conversion is

impossible at this stage. This person thinks with pride and
shores up his beliefs with pride. He knows better than anyone.
Discernment is out of the picture. What prevails is the will of
the prideful person (*Inst.* XII).

There are two kinds of pride. Spiritual pride is that which
is turned toward God. It is the sin of the proficient, of a being
which has advanced to great stages of enlightenment but who
ultimately turns toward the self and away from God, in a radical defiance. The other kind of pride, carnal pride, is more
common. It is described as a smaller measure of self-willed defiance. Beginners are afflicted with the thought of carnal pride.

About spiritual pride: the thought of pride that is turned
toward God is more serious than common offenses such as
indifference, ingratitude, or lukewarmness. Audacious thoughts
that are actually "against God" represent an end stage of a spiritual disease. The symptoms of this end stage shows themselves
in hatred of God. Thoughts against God that pride stimulates
follow this sequence: I have powers, even spiritual ones. I can
use them for my benefit. God no longer deserves my loyalty. In
fact, other seekers should be loyal to me. I can show them a
path to great heights of wisdom and power. God may not exist.
He has no power to punish those who have figured this out, like
I have. God can be damned for all I care. Hell, damnation and
punishment don't exist either. If God is good, he won't punish,
and if He does then I don't want any part of that either.

This is end-stage defiance because this is the same person
who renounced his or her former way of life, then his or her
interior thoughts that are not toward God, and now is renouncing even God.

This *train of thoughts* seriously endangers the spiritual
journey: I have fasted, been chaste, made total renunciation
of things, practiced vigilance of thoughts, manifestation of
thoughts, meditations, prayers, and manual labor, all the
spiritual practices. I am the same person who has given over

his or her life to God. My story usually shows that I have not checked vainglory, however. The experience of being awakened was simply too overwhelming. In a mysterious, destructive decision of my will, I fell off the edge and lost the struggle, ending my spiritual journey toward union with God. Pride returns me to my own self with a more powerful grip than ever. I had handed over my whole self to God, then took it all back. I now have only one reference point, "me." Where there was once prayer without ceasing, and mindfulness of the presence of God, now there is only self-adoration, as if I were God.

About carnal pride: the second kind of pride afflicts each one of us. Carnal pride gives me thoughts of exaggerated self-importance. My reference is constantly my own innermost thoughts, desires, and passions, not God. I simply live for myself. This kind of pride shows in each of my thoughts. In reference to food, for instance, I simply don't share it. Often pride is revealed in lust or avarice. I seduce someone for my own pleasure, or I grasp things greedily without consideration of how much is enough, and what other people might need. Anger may manifest my disgust that I didn't get the honor I deserve. "I am above this or that." I put others down. Acedia finds me devoting to self the time I formerly used in spiritual practices. I may think, "Living is simply too much effort, let alone keeping up my prayer life." So, carnal pride, as we see, is the collapse of the training of my thoughts, and a return to myself. God's word isn't so much defied, as forgotten and dismissed. It is "not for me." What makes carnal pride different from spiritual pride is that the self takes precedence over God. It does not lift itself up to be God as does spiritual pride.

John Cassian emphasizes over and over that pride is the most destructive thought, since it can destroy all of the virtues. It attacks the whole person. It is not content to damage a part like a leg or an arm, but casts down the whole body, mind, and soul. We have been taught that gluttony destroys temperance, lust stains purity, and anger destroys patience. Sometimes we fall into a vice, but can preserve other virtues. But pride has the capacity to destroy the whole person and strip the soul of all virtue.

Consider the myth of the Archangel Lucifer, who basked in God's glory. By his own will he transformed himself into a devil, because he thought glory was his, acquired by his own virtue. He puffed himself up and believed he had no need of divine assistance to sustain his state of purity. He esteemed himself to be like God, and like God, felt he had no need of anyone. Lucifer, the myth goes on to say, believed he was the epitome of virtue and could perpetuate perfect bliss. The fall of the angels and the subsequent downfall of holy men and women stems inevitably from pride. Pride is pervasive. Its evil is so great that the proud one makes God himself the adversary. How great pride is! There is no angel or virtue to oppose it. Other sins oppose other men, but pride takes on God.

What does pride look like? How can pride be detected? Let's look at another description from Cassian (*Inst.* XII: 27): One symptom is that our religious fervor is lukewarm. Most monks afflicted with carnal pride have not fully renounced their former way of life and find disobedience more to their liking. They are rough, not gentle and kindly. They consider themselves above their peers. Or if they are below their peers, they think themselves insulted. They are incensed at being treated as a normal mortal. Resentment prevails among them because religious life has stripped these monastics of creature comforts, and instead of feeling free and blessed, they are depressed because of being deprived of worldly goods. In their daily lives they have no practice of fasting or denying self. If they come into gifts they keep things for self gain. Their eyes are dead; their hearts are dull. Affect is flat. Socially they are takers, not givers.

The progression goes from bad to worse, says Cassian, as he describes a prideful monk: Avarice sets in and the monastic collects what he never had before. All efforts to change he finds hopeless. All restraint collapses. Cassian goes on to say that this prideful monk is impertinent and shows diabolical scorn toward his superior, to whom he should be accountable. Cassian describes his outward gait, his loud voice, his bitter silence, his mirth which is noisy and excessive, and his unreasonably gloomy mood. Cassian notes that the proud monk speaks with authority, answers with rancor, is too free with his tongue, waits not with his words, and lacks patience and charity. While he freely insults others, he is faint-hearted in bearing insults himself. He is troublesome in obedience, except when he gets a self-serving order, and is unforgiving in receiving admonition. He is weak in giving up wishes, and stubborn about yielding to others, always seeking his own ends. He is never ready to give up his own preferences for others, and he can't give sound advice because he prefers his own opinion to that of the elders (*Inst.* XII: 28).

What is most disconcerting about pride is the way it can inspire one to approach others in an attractive, spiritually seductive manner. Often, a monk who has grown cold by pride, will want to lead other people. He is skillful in making them do his will, since he feels his decisions are impeccable.

Can the monk overcome pride? To do so he must reverse the portrait described above. The prideful monk who, by the grace of God, attains compunction of heart and realizes he's been moving in the wrong direction needs to return to his best self and to start once again to control his thoughts. He must pick up once again the practice of *lectio divina* and listen with the ear of his heart to the word of God directed straight at his center.

We read that God does not call us anything less than a friend and that an abiding relationship with Christ is always available to us (Jn 15). Through prayer and fasting I realize that I cannot obtain perfect virtue and promised bliss only by my own strength All is from God. The "good thief," who died alongside Jesus at Golgotha is in each of us. I know that he responded to God's grace and that at his last hour he was admitted to paradise. There is hope for me, no matter how much distance I have traveled from my first intention to seek God. It is comforting to know that no matter how difficult the journey, it is worth it. Sorrows vanish like smoke.

How can I acquire purity of heart even after consenting to thoughts of pride? The desert fathers and mothers remind me that the answer is that God helps those who exert their will and run, seek, ask, and knock. God's mercy is available. God desires our sanctification.

When monastics take vows, the prayer after reciting the vow formula is this chant, called the Suscipe:

Accept me, Lord, according to your word, that I can live
And let me not be confounded in my expectation.

The Suscipe, is a petition to be faithful, to complete the journey during this lifetime, for the sake of life now, and in eternity. The promise holds for all of us. The path is to respond to each small inclination toward being more loving.

From whom can we learn this? We should listen to teachers, though we need to notice if they have compunction for their faults. Wholesome sorrow for sin and longing for God, being loving towards all God's creatures, should increase as purity of soul advances. Real teachers take no credit for themselves. Listen to teachers who willingly take up the spiritual journey and consent to the subtle voice of divine assistance in the deepest parts of their souls. By their fruits you will know them. Observable fruits of progress on the spiritual journey are charity, compassion, humility, and graciousness.

Don't be deceived by gray-headed elders. If you notice that they have not tamed their thoughts of food, sex, things, anger, dejection, acedia, vainglory, and pride, then they are disqualified from transmitting the tradition to you. Elders should practice what they teach. It is very clear that discernment cannot come through those who are afflicted themselves. If you notice a high degree of compunction, humility, and charity, then, listen to that sage. Ask God for strength to practice in his name. When my practices are in rhythm, my proficiency will protect me as a shield. My response to the divine action in my soul is habitual compunction, an unction that safeguards me against the thought of pride. If I remember my failings daily and long for God, my seeking will continue in humble, not self-righteous thoughts (*Conf.* II.13).

This is the simple faith of the ancient fathers. Such a faith can't be learned through dialectical syllogisms or the eloquence of a Cicero. It is learned through the experience of a pure life, stainless actions, correction of faults, and, especially, by the grace of God (*Conf.* XIV.14). The whole of *Conference* XIV is dedicated to the theme of spiritual knowledge.

Cassian admonishes that striving for perfection through my own efforts but leaving God out is the sin of blasphemy. This is so serious for one who has renounced one's former way of life, then renounced even his or her thoughts and maybe even thoughts of God; to then renounce God is a major setback in the spiritual journey. This sin leads to temptations, especially against chastity. Cassian goes on to note that one of the first disciplines to break down is chastity. I see no reason to restrain my sexual desires if there is no one except myself to whom I am accountable. I can discern, judge, and take action on my own, without considering other factors. For a prideful person, experience is the norm. Sex is the most natural expression of the self and is therefore an easily accessible activity. But it is possible also to use sex to exploit the body, sometimes using mystical language in an exaggerated way to justify ordinary sexual activity.

The perfection that is sought in pride can only be obtained by humility. Humility stands in stark relief to pride. It is neither *up* as in vainglory, nor *down* as in dejection. It is the fruit of working through acedia. I do manual labor mindfully, conscious of the presence of God, present to each moment. In the lap of humility, I am able to notice my thoughts, and can sort out which ones are from myself, which from the devilish inclinations in my unconscious mind, and which from God. Cassian tells us that humility destroys pride. To come to humility, I must first of all start once again to renounce my possessions. I must see things as only for my use, not as possessions. All is gift. As a first step, I must rededicate myself to the teaching on things. Cassian reminds the monk about the symbol of the clothing given him when he entered the monastery. He has given everything away. He is starting a new life, like an infant at baptism, who receives the symbolic white garment. He is clothed with humility and simplicity.

Cassian notes that, sadly, most people afflicted by pride do not want to be rid of it because it feels so good to be so right. Part of the end stage of pride is that the afflicted one feels sacrosanct. He has no need for repentance, conversion, or change of heart.

Sister Catherine Howard translates St. Benedict's chapter seven on humility into contemporary language: Humility requires continual reverent mindfulness of God. Being watchful over our behavior and our inner thoughts, we desire to live in harmony with God's will. We must develop a willingness to respond to others' legitimate desires and commands out of love for God and with a quiet acceptance of the necessary suffering in life. We must not succumb to life's struggles with anger, depression, and the desire to run away. It is wise to seek a mature and trusted "other" to honestly reveal our inner thoughts, good and bad. By doing so, we can even learn to be content with shabby treatment by others and be able to find a sincere, peaceful acknowledgment in our heart that we are no better, and could very well be worse than others. This ability to live in community without the compulsion to project our unique identity by acting contrary to others, shows itself in our ability to refrain from speaking on every topic, in every situation. We avoid silly, sarcastic, and demeaning laughter, and have a simple, gentle, authentic self-presentation with a quiet, nonostentatious bodily demeanor.[1] This description of humility provides a daily examination of conscience for those of us who want to practice the spirituality of this desert tradition in the twenty-first century. While the list reads easily, it takes a lifetime to enter into this way of life wholeheartedly.

Another view of the Twelve Steps of Humility are in St. Bernard of Clairvaux's *Ladder of Pride*.[2] You can notice how far along you are on the path of humility by noticing your degrees of pride. The first step is *curiosity*. The perverse person, St. Bernards says, "winks the eye, nudges the foot, points the finger" (49). The person seems to be unfocused and to go where the fancy leads. There is no guard of the heart. This leads to *levity of mind*, the second step, where the mind is tossed up and down. This leads to the third degree which is *giddiness*. This kind of raucous laughter is "at people" and is forgetful of a person's vulnerabilities. The fourth step, which is *boasting*, comes soon after that :

> You bring forth from your treasury old things and new. You are not shy about producing your opinions, words are bubbling over. You do not wait to be asked. Your information comes before any question. You ask the questions, give the answers,

---

1. Katherine Howard, O.S.B., *Praying with Benedict: Companions on the Journey* (Winona, Minn.: St. Marys Press, 1996), 81.

2. Bernard of Clairvaux, *A Lover Teaching the Way of Love*, trans. M. Basil Pennington (Hyde Park, N.Y.: New City Press, 1997), 43–51.

cut off anyone who tries to speak. When the time comes and
it is necessary to interrupt the conversation, hour-long though
it be, you seek a minute more. You must get leave to resume
your talk, not to edify your listeners, but to show off your learning. You even brag about your humility!

The fifth step is *to be singular*: You might eat more or eat
less, but always more extreme than anyone else. This delusion
exhibits itself in small matters of dress, food, gait in walking,
or conversation. Your own intention is hidden from your
heart. The sixth step is *self-conceit*, wherein you believe in
your innermost heart that you are holier than others. It's an
easy step then into *presumption*. You soon put yourself first
before anyone else. You disdain ordinary tasks as being
beneath your dignity. Faults are hidden, if corrected you make
excuses which lead to the eighth step of pride: *self justification*.

The ninth is to make a *hypocritical confession*—as a way
out: "Their eyes are cast down, they humble themselves to the
very dust." They wring out some tears if they can, sighs and
groans interrupt their words. They will not merely admit what
has happened but will exaggerate their guilt. Their protesta-
tions are a fraudulent way to offset a meaningful penance or
reparation for wrongdoing.

The tenth step is *outright revolt*. Such persons have contempt for their brothers and sisters and now show insolence
toward legitimate authorities. The eleventh step of pride is a
freedom to sin. With fewer qualms they happily give themselves
up to their sinful desires—moving step by step closer to sin.
And finally there is the habit of *sinning itself*, which is the
twelfth step of pride. The pleasure of sin becomes enjoyable
and new ways are sought to serve every impulse. One thing
leads to another.

The just who have climbed all the steps of humility by
checking and letting go of these degrees of pride within

themselves can make the shift and reverse the slide into pride, climbing the ladder of humility instead, as St. Benedict outlines in chapter seven of his Rule. They move on to life with a ready heart and with the ease of good habit. But those who have dropped down to the bottom are ruled by evil habit and, unchecked by fear, they run boldly on to death. Apathy ignores warning signals. Security is found in truth or in blindness. Fear of God has been lost and is replaced by contempt (60).

Pride deters me from the spiritual journey. If I am fortunate enough to recognize it and repent, I must start once again with the first renunciation. I renounce my former way of life, though this time I see that the motivation for that way of life was carnal pride. I see that my negative thoughts of food and drink, of sex, of things, of anger, of dejection, of acedia, and of vainglory were all expressions of my willfulness. I begin again, as if I were a first time novice on the spiritual journey, devoting myself to all the practices: silence, fasting, ceaseless prayer, guard of the heart, watchfulness of thoughts, guard of the heart, manifestation of thoughts, using my cell, *lectio divina*, vigils, manual labor, ministry, discernment, and meditation. A good starting place for reawakening is to clean out things. For instance, it would be wise to put my disposition toward things, shown in the condition of my cell, in order.

This lifestyle demanded by the middle way of renunciation is for the sake of prayer, for the sake of a relationship with Christ. The relinquishing of self-chatter in order to create a rich inner life of prayer, an intimate and wholehearted love of Christ, is as natural, easy, and normal as any intimate relationship. As a practice, the contemplative stance is simply a profound listening, accompanied by a willing, supple attraction toward all that is holy in this life and the next.

There are three guides on the spiritual journey: the Scriptures, tradition, and my elders. In these times, many of us live without elders. However, we still have the Scriptures and tradition, which can lead us to the practice of *lectio divina*, listening to the Scriptures with the heart. If I do *lectio divina* with the Scriptures, and study the sacred writings from tradition, such as those found in the desert tradition we have been examining, I will arrive at teachings I can practice with confidence. I will measure myself against the example of Christ and the saints who imitated Christ. When I know Christ in the inner heart, I will arrive at the happy place where I no longer need the constant practice of the eight thoughts.

Christians report two predominant experiences at this stage. They either talk of a love sealed by friendship and inner dialogue, even to the extent of mystical union; or they describe an abiding presence of God, undifferentiated but described universally as touching the deepest level of consciousness. This stage is often called illumination—there is the light of knowing God and the mystery of unknowing at the same time. Both experiences immerse the individual into the cosmic Christ who saturates the universe. Such a God-consciousness makes language useless. Glimpsing the true reality of God's love makes return to ordinary thought impossible. The first fruit of overcoming pride is a heart capable of meeting God "face to face." Earthly time is dedicated to loving God through *the path of unknowing*. If I am a serious seeker and I know my thoughts and renounce them, however, God as God emerges. The spiritual senses open and awareness awakens.

What are the spiritual senses? To understand the spiritual senses I must open myself to making the third renunciation. I must let go of my thoughts, even my thoughts about God, so that the spiritual senses can provide a language for a new consciousness within me. The spiritual senses are love's way of knowing God; love's way to see, feel, smell, taste, or touch God. The spiritual senses of all baptized Christians were opened during their baptismal rite:

While the ears are being signed, the celebrant says:
Receive the cross on your ears, that you may hear the voice of the Lord.
While the eyes are being signed:
Receive the sign of the cross on your eyes, that you may see the glory of God.
While the lips are being signed:
Receive the sign of the cross on your lips, that you may respond to the word of God.
While the shoulders are being signed:
Receive the sign of the cross on your shoulders, that you may bear the gentle yoke of Christ.
While the feet are being signed:
Receive the sign of the cross on your feet, that you may walk in the way of Christ.[3]

We all have the capacity to awaken our spiritual senses. Few saints talk about the experience of their spiritual senses, but awakened Christians manifest this spiritual attentiveness and thrive simply on being alive. I do not make the middle renunciation—the renunciation of thoughts which we have been talking about in this book—until I have first renounced my former life. And I make the middle renunciation before I prepare to renounce my idea of God. It purifies me so that I see what has been there all along. No obstacles remain, no duplicity. There is only God. And though I have presented the three renunciations in sequence, at some mysterious level all three renunciations must be done daily and simultaneously.

Mary Mrozowski, one of the founding mothers of the Centering Prayer movement, said, "No thought is worth thinking about." Was she talking about the fleetingness of

---

3. *Rite of Christian Initiation of Adults,* National Conference of Catholic Bishops (New York: Catholic Book Publishing Co., 1988), 28–29.

time, about how thoughts often bypass present awareness? Or was she saying that friendship with God, who is beyond thought, is infinitely preferable? I think "no thought worth thinking about" means all of the above and more. No matter which thought it is, whether of food, sex, or things, the same response is fitting: lay it aside and remember God. The grace to lay aside all thoughts other than the Beloved is a treasure from the dessert bequeathed to all of us. Deep relationships rest beyond thoughts. If we let God be God in our innermost life, then thoughts don't matter after all.

Appendix

Monastic Practices:
An Alphabetical Collection

✜ **Ceaseless prayer** is to continuously breathe the Jesus Prayer or another prayer so that the prayer acts like a mantra always working on one's consciousness at a deeper level for the sake of union with God. In learning it, the first phase is mechanical, the second mental, and the third is mystical.

✜ **The cell** is a place to practice. This space is where one finds time to be alone with God.

✜ **Compunction** is the desire for God that has the double tension of longing for God and the angst of being at a distance from him because of one's own condition.

✜ **Discernment** is the practice of listening to one's thoughts, sorting the ones that are from God, self, of the devil. The practice is to lay aside one's thoughts. Listen to that still small voice, notice a sign of confirmation, and see the fruit in one's life, e.g., love of enemies.

✜ **Fasting** is the practice of following the middle way about food and drink. One should not eat too much or too little, or eat food too high in quality or too low in nutrition. One should eat at the appropriate time. Only the needs of hospitality should be the exception.

✤ **Good zeal** is the way to do all the practices. Good zeal is thought, word, and deed all toward charity, toward the loving of others. To love others as Christ has first loved us.

✤ **Guard of the heart** is the practice of anticipating people, places, and things that are the occasion for foreign matter entering the heart that seeks to be with God.

✤ **Lectio divina,** the practice of listening with the heart to the revelatory text of Scripture, nature, or experience for the purpose of loving God. Attention to the literal and symbolic senses of the text takes time and practice and loving attention.

✤ **Manifestation of thoughts** is the practice of checking one's train of thoughts by presenting them to an elder, one who is hopefully more enlightened than yourself. The purpose is to practice humility and to stop the cyclic thinking that reoccurs in one's consciousness. This practice leads to discernment so one can sort thoughts, both intentions and objectifications. In the desert times the elder would give a word of salvation or a teaching that would impart to the disciple a grace to move beyond the affliction of the present moment.

✤ **Manual labor** is repetitive tasks to do while practicing mantric prayer. Works that reduce ego engagement. Works that give the *time* to *know* one's thoughts.

✤ **Practice of the Presence of God** is the use of active memory in ordinary consciousness using daily activities such as manual labor, personal maintenance, and natural signs to evoke habitual Christ consciousness.

✤ **Recollection** is the practice of mindfulness, being in the presence of God.

✤ **Silence** is the practice of stilling one's own thoughts and listening.

✤ **Watchfulness of thoughts** is the practice of being aware of thoughts as they come and go. It is to catch the impulses before they develop into the chain of thoughts, desires, and passions. With practice one can learn to consent to the thoughts desirable for the spiritual life. We are not our thoughts!

Select Bibliography

Allen, Diogenes. *Spiritual Theology: The Theology of Yesterday for Spiritual Help Today*. Cambridge: Cowley Publications, 1997.

Anonymous. *The Way of a Pilgrim and The Pilgrim Continues His Way*. Trans. Helen Bacovin. New York: Image Books Doubleday, 1992.

Athanasius. *Vita Antonii: The Life of Anthony and the Letter to Marcellinus*. Trans. R. C. Gregg. New York: Paulist Press, 1980.

Bernard of Clairvaux. *A Lover Teaching the Way of Love*. Trans. M. Basil Pennington. Hyde Park, N.Y.: New City Press, 1997.

Benedict. *The Rule of St. Benedict*. Ed. T. Fry. Collegeville, Minn.: The Liturgical Press, 1981. In Latin and English with notes.

Bondi, Roberta. *To Love as God Loves: Conversations with the Early Church*. Philadelphia: Fortress Press, 1987.

Brown, Peter. *The Body and Society: Men, Women, and Sexual Renunciation in Early Christianity*. New York: Columbia University Press, 1988.

———. *Augustine of Hippo: A Biography*. Berkeley and Los Angeles: University of California Press, 1969.

Burton-Christie, Douglas. *The Word in the Desert*. New York: Oxford University Press, 1993.

Casey, Michael. *Toward God*. Liguori, Mo.: Triumph Books, 1996

———. *Sacred Reading*. Liguori, Mo.: Triumph Books, 1996.

Cassian, John. *Collationes. Conferences*. Trans. Edgar C. S. Gibson. A *Select Library of Nicene and Post-Nicene Fathers*, n.s., 11. Oxford: Parker and Co., 1894. Reprint, Grand Rapids, Mich.: Eerdmans, 1989.

———. *John Cassian: Conferences*. Trans. Colum Luibheid. New York: Paulist Press, 1985.

———. *Cassian on Chastity Introduction (Institute 6, Conference 12, Conference 22)*. Trans. Terrence G. Kardong. Richardton, N.Dak.: Abbey Press, 1993.

———. *The Conferences*. Trans. O. P. Boniface Ramsey. Mahwah, N.J.: Paulist, 1997.

Catholic Catechism of the Catholic Church. Trans. United States Catholic Conference, Inc. Liguori, Mo.: Liguori Publications, 1994.

Cummings, Charles, O.C.S.O. *Monastic Practices*. Cistercian Studies no. 75. Kalamazoo, Mich.: Cistercian Publications, 1986.

Driscoll, Jeremy, O.S.B. *The "Ad Monachos" of Evagrius Ponticus: The Monks Long Journey To The Holy Trinity*. Collegeville, Minn.: The Liturgical Press, 1993.

Dalai Lama, H. H. *The Policy of Kindness*. Ithaca, N.Y.: Snow Lion Publications, 1993.

Epstein, Mark, M. D. *Thoughts Without a Thinker*. New York: Basic Books Harper Collins Publishers, 1995.

Evagrius Ponticus. *The Practikos and Chapters on Prayer*. Trans. John Eudes Bamberger. Kalamazoo, Mich.: Cistercian Publications, 1978.

Goettmann, Alphonse and Rachel. *The Spiritual Wisdom and Practices of Early Christianity*. Trans. Theodore J. Nottingham. Greenwood, Ind.: Inner Life Publications, 1994.

Hausherr, Irenee, S.J., *Penthos: The Doctrine of Compunction in the Christian East*. Trans. Anselm Hufstader, O.S.B. Kalamazoo, Mich.: Cistercian Publications, 1982.

————. *The Name of Jesus*. Trans. Charles Cummings, O.C.S.O. Cistercian Studies no. 44. Kalamozoo, Mich.: Cistercian Publications, 1978.

Historia Monachorum in Aegypto. Trans. Norman Russell. *The Lives of the Desert Fathers*. Introd. Benedicta Ward. London: Mowbray, 1980.

James, Stuart, ed. *Swami Abhishiktananda: His Life Told through His Letters*. Delhi: Indian Society for Promoting Christian Knowledge (ISPCK), 1995.

Kardong, Terrence. *Benedict's Rule: A Translation and Commentary*. Collegeville, Minn.: Liturgical Press, 1996.

Keating, Thomas, O.C.S.O. *Open Mind, Open Heart: The Contemplative Dimension of the Gospel*. New York: Warwick: Amity House, 1986.

Leclercq, Jean, O.S.B. *The Love of Learning and the Desire for God*. New York: Fordham University Press, 1961.

Louf, Andre. "Spiritual Fatherhood in the Literature of the Desert." In *Abba*. Ed. John R. Sommerfeldt. Kalamazoo, Mich.: Cistercian Publications, 1982.

Lives of Pachomius. Trans. Armand Veilleux. *Pachomian Koinonia: The Lives, Rules, and Other Writings of Saint Pachomius and His Disciples,* vol.1. *The Life of Saint Pachomius and His Disciples.* Cistercian Studies no. 45. Kalamazoo, Mich.: Cistercian Publications, 1980.

Maloney, George, ed. *Pilgrimage of the Heart: A Treasury of Eastern Christian Spirituality.* San Francisco: Harper & Row, 1983.

McGinn, Bernard. *Foundations of Mysticism.* New York: Crossroad, 1991.

———. *The Presence of God: A History of Western Christian Mysticism.* New York: Crossroad, 1994.

Merton, Thomas. "The Spiritual Father in the Desert Tradition." Cistercian Studies, no. 3, 1968.

———. *The Wisdom of the Desert.* New York: New Directions, 1960.

———. *Zen and the Birds of Appetite.* New York: New Directions, 1968.

———. *Mystics and Zen Masters.* New York: The Noonday Press, 1967.

———. *The Climate of Monastic Prayer.* Kalamazoo, Mich.: Cistercian Publications, 1969.

Mitchell, Donald and James Wiseman, ed. *The Gethsemani Encounter.* New York: Continuum Publishing Group, 1997.

Monastic Interreligious Dialogue Bulletin. Ed. James Conner. Since 1978 published three times a year from Ky.: Abbey of Gethsemani

Norris, Kathleen. *Cloister Walk.* Boston: Riverhead Publishers, 1996.

Nouwen, Henry. *The Way of the Heart.* New York: Ballantine Books, 1981.

Palladius. *The Lausiac History (Historia Lausiaca) of Paladius.* Trans. Robert T. Meyer. *The Lausiac History.* Westminister, Md.: Newman Press, 1965.

Philokalia: The Complete Text, vol. 1–4. Ed. St. Nikodimos of Holy Mountain and St. Makarios of Corinth. Trans. G. E. H. Palmer, Philip Sherrard, and Kallistos Ware. England: Faber and Faber, 1995.

———. *Prayer of the Heart: Writings from the Philokalia.* Trans. G. E. H. Palmer, Philip Sherrard, and Kallistos Ware. Boston: Shabhala, 1993.

Patanjali Yoga Sutras: How to Know God. Trans. Swami Prabhavananda published by the President, Sri Ramakrishna Math. Mylapore, Madras, 1997.

Schneiders, Sandra. "Scripture and Spirituality." In *Christian Spirituality: Origins to the Twelfth Century*. Ed. Bernard McGinn, J. Meyendorff, and Jean Leclercq. New York: Fortress Press, 1985.

―――. *The Relevatory Text*. San Francisco: Harper, 1991.

Spidlik, Thomas. *The Spirituality of the Christian East: A Systematic Handbook*. Trans. A. P. Gythiel. Kalamazoo, Mich.: Cistercian Publications, 1986.

Sophrony, Archimandrite. *The Monk of Mount Athos*. Trans. Rosemary Edmonds. Crestwood, N. Y.: St. Vladimir's Seminary Press, 1989.

Stewart, Columba, O.S.B. *Cassian the Monk*. New York: Oxford University Press, 1998.

Underhill, Evelyn. *Mysticism: A Study in the Nature and Development of Man's Spiritual Consciousness*. New York: New American Library, 1974.

―――. *Mystics of the Church*. Harrisburg, Penn., 1925.

Ward, Benedicta. "Signs and Wonders: Miracles in the Desert Tradition." *Studia Patristics*, 17. 1982.

―――. *The Sayings of the Desert Fathers: The Alphabetical Collection*. London: Mowbrays, 1975.

―――. *The Wisdom of the Desert Fathers: Apophthegmata Patrum from the Anonymous Series*. Oxford: SLG Press, 1975.

Ware, Kallistos. *The Power of the Name*. Oxford: Fairacres, 1974.

―――. "Pray without Ceasing: The Ideal of Continual Prayer in Eastern Monasticism." *Eastern Churches Review*, 2. 1969.